Lube of Life

A Tribute to Sex, Love, and the Pursuit of Happiness in the Boomer Age

Mindy Mitchell & Edward Land

Turn the Page
PUBLISHING

Published by Turn the Page Publishing LLC
P. O. Box 3179
Upper Montclair, NJ 07043
www.turnthepagepublishing.com

ISBN-13: 978-1-938501-14-2

ISBN ebook-13: 978-1-938501-15-9

Lube of Life
Library of Congress Control Number 2012950542

PRINTED IN THE UNITED STATES OF AMERICA

Editor R.S. Lentin

Cover Design by Robin McGeever, McB Design

DEDICATIONS

Mindy to Edward:
Thank you for agreeing to be my training wheels!

Edward to Mindy:
Thank you for asking!

INTRODUCTIONS

MINDY:
How it all began

I owe the documentation of this charming, mid-life love story to my dear sweet Edward, who has an uncanny tendency to document things in chronological format, which is how our on- and off-line dating timeline came to be preserved.

There are several formats contained herein: closed e-mails through the dating site where we initially met, online chatting through the dating site, personal e-mails (once we got to know each other better), phone texts, and live phone conversations.

Communication within these venues occurred many times during the course of a day . . . or even an hour. As anyone who has dated online can tell you, time speeds up with so much sharing of thoughts within these formats, but I know that it is not as rapid as it appears in these pages.

CHAPTER 1

MINDY:

Online Dating (One more try!)

I'm angry. I never expected to be this person at this time in my life: alone and seeking someone via the Internet. Over the years, I have sporadically used online match sites and each time I gave up in frustration, most of the time with myself. Looking at how others see me makes me focus on how I see myself. It is a vicious loop of sadness, hope, frustration, embarrassment, grandiosity and feeling less than. Emotional whiplash at its finest.

My strong feelings surprise me and illuminate the fact that I may, indeed, have some "issues" (self-esteem leaps to mind) around this whole thing.

After 59+ years of being on this earth and two marriages, you would think I would be better equipped to find a lasting and loving connection with the opposite sex. Not so much.

Thinking about embarking on yet another quest for a committed relationship naturally brings to mind relationships of the past. I haven't had many … except for that spate of encounters in the '70s when I wasn't really attached to anyone in particular. It seemed like the thing to do at the time. Anyway.

Regarding online dating: for every success story there seems to be an endless litany of horror stories. It only makes sense when one is trying to find the proverbial "partner in a haystack." If nothing else, this whole experiment in terror made me look at myself, my foibles and my hasty generalizations based on a stranger's picture and their few written words.

After some thought, I decide upon *ClarityNow* as my online

moniker. I hope this "handle" would attract a similar soul on a like-minded journey, even if I don't really know what that means. One thing is for certain, I need all the clarity I can get when it comes to this process of online dating.

Despite my misgivings, I was compelled to try one more time; so, I sign on for another 6-month stint. Strap me in. Shoot me now.

I put pen to paper, struggle to subdue my internal critic (lest I invite in someone with a similar critical bent), compose my profile, squinch my eyes, hit SEND, and hope for the best!

EDWARD:

Finally, I am taking my own advice! I went online to find the right woman for me; hopefully, the woman who would be at my side for the rest of my life.

I have liked girls for as long as I can remember. I guess I was five-years-old when I learned there was a physical difference between boys and girls. It didn't particularly mean anything to me at the time. When I was eight, I had a friend who was a girl and I enjoyed visiting with her as much as with my guy friends. When the guys accused me of having a girlfriend, I wasn't mature enough to own it and said no, but I knew inside that it was true. I was ten when my father finally clued me in to what the difference was good for. This knowledge was not in time to prevent me losing my fifth grade girlfriend to an older, more knowing fellow. She broke my heart. But I still liked the company of the ladies. In my teens, the accusation of having a girlfriend was met with a proud "Heck, yeah!" There was not always a girlfriend in my life, but if not, I had my eyes open and my ear to the ground.

One thing I decided was to not get married too young. So, I loved a few good women over some years. Not as many as I would have liked, but all in all, I am blessed.

When I met my future wife at age 31, I had known enough women to not feel like I had missed out on the variety and spice of life, and I was ready to commit. I was 33 when I got married and 35 when I became a father. I was with my wife for 22 years. The last eleven years had been a downward spiral of declining health for her. The doctors never did determine what her ailment was. She ultimately died of heart failure.

About a year after my wife's untimely death, I found a connection with the mom of one of my son's friends. From the beginning of our relationship, we discussed the fact that we lived very different lifestyles and were not sure how far we could/would go. That conversation was revisited about once a year. We shared an excellent five years and then she withdrew. That was a year ago.

So now, with 60 years of life and experience, I find myself without the company of one good special woman, and I am lonely.

While checking my e-mail one evening, I see an ad for a mature meeting site, and decide to go exploring. I wound up joining, paying my money, and start looking around. At first I'm looking around the country, started literally the whole country, until I learn how to do a focused search. At the top of my wish list is proximity, a lady who lives close to me. Let's be practical. It really is counterproductive to find the perfect woman, only to discover that she lives too far away to become an integral part of my life.

I write my profile in one sitting and get most of the information

I thought essential included. It's more of a philosophical, emotional, spiritual presentation. I list my interests, but don't really spell out what kind of woman I'm looking for, other than of similar age and experience. I post a couple passable pictures to get started and add a few more shortly thereafter. I want to see what the ladies look like, physiques as well as smiles, and I'm sure the interest is mutual. Let's make it easy on everyone and play an accurate game of show and tell … emphasis on accurate. That concept seems to be mostly my silly little personal desire. I've always preferred to undersell myself. Then, if I am "mo betta" than you expected, you would be pleasantly surprised instead of disappointed, as I was too often after meeting someone in person.

MINDY'S ONLINE PROFILE

A little about me...

I am an enthusiastic learner and curious by nature. Self-sufficient, caring, sincere, trustworthy and honest to a fault. I have my foibles but have ironed out quite a few issues and, am willing to look at and work on the rest. We're all on a path and mine has been interesting, life-changing and worthy of the time. Love to share in laughter, travel, and find my work exciting and challenging. Who knew?

About the one I'm looking for...

I am looking for someone who is forthright, honest, and fun to be around with a sense of humor and wonder at what lies ahead. Natural curiosity and kindness. The ability to be close but not clingy. Capable of stringing a few words/sentences together and sharing openly. Oh, and kissing for days...

I'd just like to add...

I keep fit, eat well, laugh a lot, travel, help others and would enjoy doing that with a partner. Growing together, and sharing experiences...there is nothing better.

Mindy

Perhaps

I am thinking it would be beyond amazing to find a fellow traveler for the second half of my life. And is it too much to ask, all things considered, that he be a great kisser, too? My life has been lacking in that particular area and, as long as I am compiling a wish list, I might as well put that at the top of my requirements. Don't judge.

As I idly scroll through photos (the "teasers" that get you to stop at profiles and read more) my attention is caught by the visage of a smiling (well, grinning from ear to ear, actually) man, casually leaning on … something … not sure what … a bridge? And the energy of his stance and demeanor leads me to open his profile and read more about him.

EDWARD'S ONLINE PROFILE

A little about me...

I consider every day to be a blessing in the journey through life. Being alone does not mean being lonely or insufficient, simply solo, and I do that well. Yet, the journey is greatly enhanced with the company of a good and dear friend. Perhaps we will be such friends, perhaps not. Shall we begin our mutual awareness?

About the one I'm looking for...

I'm interested in meeting a smart, mature young woman (I'm a wise 30 in my mind, how about you?) of similar age and therefore, similar social awareness and references. Independence and self-sufficiency are very attractive. I want a friend and partner. Romantic, loving, touching, sharing (mind, spirit, body). I'm not a sports fan but if you are, I can go with that. (You like something, I like you, my horizons can expand.) I like spiritual but not religious. We are spiritual beings having a physical experience. Shall we share the experience?

I'd just like to add...

I wish them no harm, but I am not a pet person. The affection and company that I desire comes from a woman/friend. Part of my reality is that I have another seven years before I can retire. That means that I will be in the Tidewater, Virginia area for a while and I'm not free to go traveling about. I need/want a lady close enough (Tidewater) to visit/share with. Check the map for distance. Let's be real. Thank you very much.

I have enjoyed music all my life (eclectic taste) and want

a similar appreciation. The occasional live concert is good. Recently began learning to dance the Carolina Shag and am doing well and enjoying. "Young lady, may I have this dance?" I do not own a motorcycle now but intend to change that in the next couple years. I want a friend who likes to ride, if not (better yet) drive her own. I am a handy fellow (carpenter plus much more). I was a great husband (rest her soul) and am an excellent father (bless my son's heart).

Ladies, Please do not just Flirt with me. If you're interested, tell me something thoughtful as well. Always have a photo in your profile.

So, enough about me for a while. I apologize for monopolizing the conversation. Who, and how are You? I'm looking forward to your reply.

Edward

EDWARD:

I find it interesting that almost everyone on a dating site loves long walks on the beach, they are always on time, and they love to cuddle by the fire. My username ends up a slight comedy of errors. I ask for *MrEd* for ease of recognition and remembrance, but surprisingly, someone already has that handle. The site server suggests *FunMrEdward* and I go with it in the heat of the moment. Later, I find it frightening how many people have the word "fun" in their username. Oh well, I just need to be able to live up to my name, and I know I can.

One of the site features is "Flirts," where prefab little mindless comments can be sent out in a few seconds. Immediately, I add the request to my profile to not send just a flirt ... send a real message please. This flirting business can suck up a great deal of my time if I respond thoughtfully to each one. I believe my least favorite is "Feel Free To Contact Me." That's because these flirts, more often than not, come from people who meet none of my criteria - no photo, skeletal profiles, and sometimes illiterate. Yes, they get my attention, but not in a favorable way. If you pluck my nerve before we even share words, I'm not going there. I have things to go, places to do, womenz to meet, the woman to meet.

Another annoyance is the number of women without a picture, the faceless people, and how many of them really want to meet me. How exciting for me. Wait, you wouldn't have looked at my profile or made contact if I didn't have a picture. Why would I have any interest in looking at your profile if you don't have a picture? A person's appearance isn't the only factor in a good relationship, but it's important and I want to know before investing more time and energy.

I've been looking around the site for a couple weeks, sending and receiving "hellos." The local ladies I reach out to aren't interested in me. A few bother to let me know. Most just ignore me, never responding. Most all of the ladies reaching out to me reside at least a hundred miles away, if not more. The cuter they are and the better the alignment of our ideas and activities, the farther away they live.

A number of women with no picture say, "Send me a message ... I will tell you about myself later." I'm baffled by the number of women who seem to pay no attention to my profile parameters. They want to introduce me to their half dozen pets, take me to church, have me help raise their grandchildren, AND they only live a few hundred miles away. Not a one of those items is on my "list of things to do" but they don't have a clue why we're not a perfect match and why I'm not at their house already. Go figure. And though I add to my profile the statement that I will no longer respond to just a Flirt without a message, I can't find it in my heart to not respond to everyone. All of the wrong people tugging on my sleeve are sucking up a great deal of time and energy.

Needing a filing system, I create different folders to help me keep track of those I contact and those who contact me. I make copies of their profiles, where they were located, and keep a running log of communications. There's a folder for each of the several cities in my immediate area and a folder titled "Cute But Too Far." Of course, it's in this folder that most of the interesting appearing ladies' profiles come to be stored.

CHAPTER 2

MINDY:

I am struck by Edward's ability to express himself through writing. I sense no guile. His words ring true and sincere. He seems to have a sense of humor. And he lives 3.5 hours away and is only interested in meeting a woman in his town. Bummer.

I vacillate between wanting to contact him and leaving well enough alone. He is clear about only wanting local women to contact him. He is not free to travel as he still works and needs someone close by.

I throw caution to the wind and e-mail him anyway:

From: ClarityNow
To: FunMrEdward
Date: Thursday, July 21
Subject: Hello ...

Dear FunMrEdward:

I enjoyed your profile and believe we have many similarities in our way of thinking and appreciating life and all it has to offer. I haven't looked up the Tidewater area yet to see what our distance is. I, too, still work but am seriously looking at another re-invention of myself. I have done it quite a few times over the years and it works well for me. I am spirituality-based. And, like you, think of myself as somewhere in my 30's (until I see my reflection in a window. :-) Life is short; every day is a gift. My intention is to live this second half with a joy-filled, enthusiastic partner. I am blessed with excellent health ... who knew that would be so important down the road ... apparently, I come from hardy genetic stock!

I look forward to hearing from you,
Mindy

EDWARD:

She is easy on the eyes and her profile sounds like we would get along well, and she lives only 200 miles away. I'm busy so it takes me a couple days to see and respond to her first message.

From:	FunMrEdward
To:	ClarityNow
Date:	Saturday, July 23
Subject:	Re: Hello ...

Hello Ms. Mindy, Thank you for your message. Most intriguing. We do seem to have a good bit in common, mental, physical, and spiritual. Oh darn, how did that happen? And why is it happening so far away? Reston is about 200 miles and 3 1/2 hours away. Shucks almighty. Looking at your profile shows you to be a cutie and a sweetheart. I'm very affectionate without clinging. I'm not sure I can construct a coherent thought pattern any farther than I can throw it, but somehow I manage to get a point across. Remember, eschew obfuscation. And kissing for days, well, you are just toying with our emotions. Gotta include nights as well. (More emotional toying)

Your photos of world travels, that's just showing off (gentle humorous voice, not ugly voice), making us envious. Since traveling a little in my childhood (dad was in the Army), my only foreign travel was two years ago when I went to France to visit my half-brother, who is French. Big fun. Not enough time.

So I find myself sitting here, interested in this lady before me, and knowing that we are not going to become an item at this distance. Makes me sad. But I wish you well in your search for the man who deserves to share your time. Please be in touch about how it goes in your corner of the world. Take care and Happy Trails.

From: ClarityNow
To: FunMrEdward
Date: Saturday, July 23
Subject: Re: Hello ...

Edward,
Guess I will keep hunting and pecking in my own neck of the woods ... more's the pity ... I think we would be stunning together. :-) Best to you on your journey! Mindy

EDWARD:

She is a cutie. I like tall women and Mindy says she is 5'6". I was a carpenter and have a fair grip on measurements, though the angles of her photos make her appear shorter.

MINDY:

At some point, Edward and I inadvertently end up online simultaneously and I contact him via the dating site chat. We commence to "talk" in the moment via this texting venue. We are not in a group "chat room."

EDWARD:

This evening (Saturday), Mindy says, "Hello" through the online chat window of The Dating Site, and Lordy, do we carry on.

The Dating Site—online chat July 23, Saturday evening
FunMrEdward: Well, Hey girl! How's by you?

Claritynow: I was trying to see if the chat messages you sent were on here somewhere.

FunMrEdward: That's alright. After it seemed that you were not actually at the computer, I asked if you left it on all night, kind of like leaving the porch light on.

Claritynow: Ha-ha! Just like the motel commercials. Do you feel like I am stalking you?

FunMrEdward: Not a bit. Perhaps wishin' and hopin,' to borrow a line from Dusty Springfield. I know the feeling.

Claritynow: I realize that even though I am nothing like what you are looking for ... that is, somewhere in your neck of the woods, I do feel drawn to you so just know you are more than mental bubblegum for me.

Claritynow: Then again ... I may be assuming too much.

FunMrEdward: What, pray tell, could you be assuming?

Claritynow: Hmmm ... good question. I am feeling a visceral connection to you ... like I knew you in another life (the '70s?!) so there is a comfort level I can't explain ... that and the whole you are cuter than cute, of course.

FunMrEdward: Girl, you know how to blow smoke up my skirt. But seriously, I feel we are kindred spirits and thus, we are comfortable together. Wonderful.

Claritynow: Yes. Not to set unrealistic expectations as, again, I am not what you are looking for in this time and place ... but so fun to run into you again. And happy we have connected even in this venue.

FunMrEdward: Yes ma'am. So, all of this ... not what I'm looking for ... stuff. Who are you trying to convince, you or me? You know that unfortunate reality, time and space. But aside from that, we seem to enjoy each other's company and I will accept what we can share. Sharing from afar isn't as fulfilling as either of us wants or deserves. But some sharing beats no sharing.

Claritynow: No convincing. I don't think. Hmmmm. Damn ... you are full of good points (!) I guess I am going on the premise of you needing to meet someone close by so you can settle in and create a life, et al ... AND you have to stay in that neck of the woods for awhile longer ... but, to your comment about sharing from afar ... well that opens up a whole other aspect of things.

Claritynow: The other point being creating a somewhat pretend relationship via e-mail and phone (not that it is always pretend but it is easier to get sidetracked from reality) and then meeting only to be disappointed ...

FunMrEdward: Well, we know that could happen. For all of the electron, distant sharing of poetry and philosophy, we could be drab together. I would be surprised, but it could be. That's why I feel it's important to quickly meet someone, so you can rub your auras together. Literally and figuratively.

Claritynow: :-p

Claritynow: That was supposed to be a smiley face ... Not sure what that is ...

FunMrEdward: It looks more like a lascivious ... lick you all over ... kind of thing. There I go, toying with my emotions and yours.

Claritynow: Ha-ha ... indeed.

CHAPTER 3

EDWARD:

In the next few days there's a flurry of The Dating Site e-mail communication, most tinged with the sad awareness that we're not going to get together. We're mutually encouraging about the dating/seeking experience and choose to approach our relationship from that perspective ... supportive buddies.

Within three days of our initial "meeting," we exchange phone numbers and personal e-mail addresses to make our visiting easier. Our conversations are all excellent in content and flow. We're equally wonky spirits with similar humors and interests. Our sharing just flows like it is supposed to between two people who are becoming romantically involved. Yet we're speaking of spiritually maintaining the distance that actually exists in miles between us.

A great deal of information can be shared with the keyboard. It's good for editing and clarifying before hitting the "Send" button. But there are no fonts with tone or feeling. Depending on the reader's perception, the intent of a sentence can be understood or misconstrued.

The telephone is another step forward in the process of getting acquainted. Hearing someone's voice, manner, timing and innuendo, all adds dimension, depth and understanding. How easily the conversation flows is a strong indicator of compatibility, in my opinion.

I realize fairly quickly after joining the The Dating Site that actually meeting someone soon after making contact is also important and helpful in determining compatibility. A complaint I heard from a couple ladies I had "met" was that some men were very intriguing at the distance of computer and/or phone, only to be revealed as two-dimensional in person. It's easy to be flamboyant at a distance. It's sometimes not so easy up close.

I'm fairly well-balanced, even keeled, and try to be my natural self in all of the venues. It really is pointless to present myself as someone or something that I'm not. If you like the person I have presented, good. Let's get better acquainted. If you don't like that person, save us both the time and trouble, and move along. No harm, no foul.

MINDY:
Red Flag?

Somehow, through various e-mails and online exchanges (in a very rapid amount of time) I felt comfortable enough to take Edward's phone number and give him a call. I believe we talked non-stop for two hours. It could have been more. It is something of a happy blur since we traipsed and tripped over more disparate topics than any two people should on an initial phone conversation.

One thing comes to light that sets me back somewhat. Edward enjoys a drink and I am a recovering alcoholic. It intrigues me how normal drinkers have no point of reference for someone who has an allergy to demon rum and needs to stay away from it. To them, it is no big deal. To me, it is my life (or lack thereof should I start drinking again).

So a conversation or, lack thereof, around this topic with Edward is an important one for me to have. And, at this time, we really have no thought of actually meeting or spending time together so it's basically a moot point.

But I did feel it necessary to impress upon him the seriousness of my recovery and its importance in my life. People who have never trod the slippery path of alcoholism and come out the other side just don't get it. And good for them. It is not a path for the faint of heart. And I am grateful every day that I am one of the ones that is staying sober, one day at a time.

EDWARD:
Sobriety

One of the things we talk about is the fact that Mindy is in recovery from alcoholism. She is approaching twenty-three years sober. I know a couple folks in the program so I have more than a passing awareness of the dilemmas of alcoholics and the people around them. I'm blessed that alcohol doesn't call my name, tugging on my sleeve. I enjoy a drink or two, but it doesn't cause me to lose hold of my responsibilities and damage my life, or other's lives.

Mindy and I realize that this difference in our two lifestyles is a potential deal breaker. Regardless of how well we were carrying on over the phone, it would remain to be seen if we could coexist peaceably and happily with this reality difference. I also think that it's easier for me to abide by her non-drinking than for her to abide my drinking. That puts the ball more in her court, though not entirely. I would like to have a lady friend with whom I can share a glass of wine, or a mixed drink with dinner. But for me, that's not a deal breaker. We'll have to share time together to find the answer to this disparity. But we're just buddies, anyway, so it isn't important for us to figure this out.

From: FunMrEdward
To: ClarityNow
Date: Sunday, July 24
Subject: Re: Hi Edward

Good Morning Mindy,
If you want to call this morning, any time up to 12 is good. Then I'm going to the YMCA to swim some laps. This afternoon, between 2:30 and 5 would work. These time-frames give us time to talk before I have to be responsible elsewhere. I concur with the ... nice to hear your voice ... reality. Speaking will be more pleasant than typing. We'll just have to do a better job of not doing it at the same time. We can do this.
Looking forward,
Edward

EDWARD:

Mindy calls me and we have a phone conversation this afternoon, a Sunday. It's the first of many phone conversations in which we explore the universe, large and small ... the universe within ourselves and around us. Her calling gives me her phone number but I don't even know her last name yet.

An early topic is Mindy's concern that I might think her to be too "woo-woo," out in space or left field with some of her beliefs and interests. Cases in point: reincarnation, affirmations of intent, karma, astrology, spirits, and ghosts. I thoroughly enjoy our discussions of these things. It's not to curry her favor because I've sincerely considered most of these things in my past intellectual travels, seeking awareness and learning of truths and events beyond myself and beyond traditional science.

Personal aside: In reference to the "currying of favor" (defined as artificially agreeing with someone in the hope of obtaining sex), I determined early in my sexual travels that seeking sex through false pretenses was a terrible idea. Fortunately, I learned this from seeing it happen to others, not myself. Then, as part of trying to be a good parent, I had counseled my son on this idea. He is a dedicated carnivore who was attracted to a young lady in his circle of friends. She's a dedicated vegan. Though he was interested in getting closer, much closer with her, I urged him not to try to pass himself off as a like-minded vegan. Soon or sooner, she would smell a cheeseburger on his breath and it wouldn't end well. It will end, but not well. Nonetheless, their relationship was short-lived.

From:	ClarityNow
To:	FunMrEdward
Date:	Sunday, July 24
Subject:	Today's chat ...

... Hi Edward :-) I SO enjoyed our conversation today. I like that you are so forthcoming and honest. I sense that you would be a very good man to know on many levels.

Having said that, my recovery and abstinence from drugs and alcohol is a life and death matter for me. You would not want to see me drunk, trust me. It has been a long time but my memory is fresh in that regard. I hope you find someone to share a glass of wine with and also who lives close enough to spend many nights with you. I envy them the experience. I hope we can stay in touch ... at least until

the women start beating a path to your door and you don't
need this site anymore.
Mindy

From: FunMrEdward
To: ClarityNow
Date: Monday, July 25
Subject: Re: Today's chat ...

Ms. Mindy, Hey sweetie. I also tremendously enjoyed our
vocal visit today. Forthcoming and honest, well that cuts
through so much stuff. Thank you for noticing. You/I
don't have to keep track of what I told to whom. Actually,
I'm not a good liar and I like that about myself. Are you
familiar with the KISS theory, "Keep It Simple, Silly." Not
to be confused with the "Kiss You All Over Reality," which
I highly recommend to everyone. If you don't want to share
that with someone, you aren't with the correct someone.
But I lapse into emotional toying, I apologize.

I'll certainly take your word about not wanting to see you
drunk. Just now, the question crossed my mind and I have
to wonder, who/what is released when you drink. Is it a
universal demon that is timeless and comes out through
any/all drunk souls? Or is it someone who was hurt/
wounded by certain persons/events and would not need to
come back if the hurts were healed?

Have you had these thoughts? Let me know how it
turns out. I think I mentioned, while we were speaking,
if you have been in recovery for 23 years and you haven't
accomplished it by now, you just aren't trying and I suggest

you have a glass of wine to relax and ponder. A glass won't release a demon. And actually, by now, the demon (if there was one) has gotten bored and moved on to someone with a lot more action going on, someone with much more venom to spew. Anyway, do what you need to do to be comfy with yourself.

The electronic path to my door is overly trodden, mostly with illiteracy, no photos and/or my grandmother ... not an attractive picture. The exceptions, like yourself (did I mention I could be warm for your form, and the rest of you too?) are at a distance. A reality check, nonfunctional distance. But I hold faith and hope, for myself and for your sweet self. Create and project the mental picture of you and your sweetie (face to be announced later). Keep projecting this image and it will come true. Yes, I would like for us to be in touch, if only through the flow of electrons, be they keyboard or phone.

So, it's past my bedtime. Sweet dreams.

Edward

CHAPTER 4

From: FunMrEdward
To: ClarityNow
Date: Tuesday, July 26
Subject: Our Ongoing Edgumacation

Hey Mindy,

I had two dates with the same woman this weekend. The first was on Friday evening. Out of that, a second on Sunday evening evolved. For whatever reason, I did not gel with her. That's fine with me because she didn't gel with me either, but I would prefer for her to say "no thanks." I can take it. I'm not sure she could. She's had a tough road but I can't fix it for her, and I'm not sure how hard she's working on that herself. Yesterday, in thinking about the weekend experience, it occurred to me that this computer dating thing allows us to meet more people that we don't like enough to want to hang out with, much less get close to. I gave myself a chuckle. Also reminded me that it's possible to meet someone we do want to get close with, and that's the point of being here. So, keep the faith Edward! Keep the faith Mindy!

Be good or don't get caught. Later. Edward

From: ClarityNow
To: FunMrEdward
Date: Tuesday, July 26
Subject: Re: Our Ongoing Edgumacation

My dear Edward,

You are a man of enlightened insight with a succinct way of expressing yourself. It's true. This whole whack-a-mole dating thing is really helping me get clear on what I do/don't want. It also makes me realize how lucky I was to not HAVE to date for quite a few years of my life. I also find it intriguing that folks our age either seem to be (1) damaged beyond repair, whether emotionally, physically or spiritually; or (2) are rather snippy because they have had to overcome so many things in their lives. Not sure which category I fit into but I would like to think, in my grandiose way, that I have learned enough lessons to not have to come back and do this again. Not sure. Couldn't swear to it.

My experience with this online dating thing, thus far, is that either one or the other datees are quite smitten while the other is just not feeling it. I have experienced it both ways. Humbling at best. Maddening at worst. But, again, it's all about honing the edges. And wishing for the best. And seeing what shows up. So, yes ... I will keep on keepin' on and see what is around the next corner. Lordy.

So, that is my 2 cents worth ... for what it's worth.   :-)

Mindy

From: FunMrEdward
To: ClarityNow
Date: Wednesday, July 27
Subject: Whack A Mole – Part 1

Hello Mindy,

I like your Whack-a-Mole comparison. We have no control over our genetic backgrounds. We can only control/affect our attitude and responses to the various wounding events, as well as uplifting events. Some folks do it better than others, lord knows why, but she's not telling.

I concur with your thoughts about having performed the life cycle well enough, learned the lessons well enough to not have to come back and do it again. I've been good. I'm sure you have. I like the concept of reincarnation. Interesting.

Are interested in what the astrologers think? I look at the info from both sides, you to me and me to you. I won't let this stuff keep me from getting out of bed in the morning, or dictate how I feel about someone. I do, however, find it interesting how accurate it tends to be, kind of a hindsight thing. You might find it interesting or helpful.

Since you shared your name and phone number we are now equally informed. Also, here is my e-mail address, if you are inclined to go there. Remember, using this will share your e-address with me.

And so lady, keep hanging in there.

Your two cents worth ... priceless. Edward

From: Mindy
To: Edward
Date: Wednesday, July 27
Subject: FYI

Edward,

I could do with a dose of your humor and wisdom, my friend. Actually, even nattering would be nice ... not that you natter ... but I've had an odd day at work and home late. So, I was thinking to give you a call tonight but it is late and I haven't eaten dinner.

I am also perturbed that you have had more dates in the past week than I have had in the past YEAR ... WTF?!

I totally need to get some dinner in me.

Mindy

From: Mindy
To: Edward
Date: Wednesday, July 27
Subject: PS.

I forgot to mention: I love your e-mails ... they brighten my day as I usually access them while I am at work and can def use the respite of your creative thinking, musings, ponderings. I am going to the astrology site now.

Well ... first I'm going to make some popcorn ... then on to the astrology site.

Have a good evening, Mindy

EDWARD:

Mindy is interested in seeing more pictures of me, so we "friend" each other on Facebook. Struggling with the photo upload process is part of my fun (NOT), but I finally get it to work, in spite of myself.

From: Edward
To: Mindy
Date: Wednesday, July 27
Subject: Scrounging for Photos

Hey Mindy, I figured out how to upload pictures ... pain in the butt, all different with this new and improved crap. This photo is from 30 years ago, just prior to cutting my hair. I went totally undercover. It's tough to find pics of myself because I'm always the person behind the camera. But I really am 6'1" and I'm Technicolor in real life, not just online. Good to speak with you this evening. Go girl. Edward

Half a lifetime ago

From: Mindy
To: Edward
Date: Thursday, July 28
Subject: Another day ...

Good morning, Edward ... excellent photos! You do, indeed, appear to be yourself. A handsome dude by all accounts. Technicolor to be sure.

Your son has great energy, too. Wonderful that you have each other.

I, too, believe that I am Technicolor in real life ... It ebbs and flows but generally I am pretty even keeled. I do feel that I am on the cusp of a big change ... not sure what that means. I am reminded of the saying, "when one door closes another opens, but it's hell standing in the hallway." I feel like I am standing in the hallway and have been for some time. Important for me to not attach my next steps to a man as I don't look to someone to save me or change my life or be my savior ... just want to be ready, willing and able to recognize him when he shows up. My expectation is that it will be effortless because it will be what is supposed to happen. Then again, on my crankier days, I just want him to get here so we can get on with things.

Do you have plans for the weekend? Come fall I will start working at home tours and open houses on the weekend. The schedule gets very hectic and tiring. So I have been enjoying doing nothing for the past few weekends.

This Saturday I am having an acupuncture treatment. This is in addition to the 4 "tune ups" I have throughout the year at the change of seasons. It keeps the meridians open and zinging on all cylinders. I am not afraid of aging (well, not much), but I do have a healthy fear of falling into ill health so try to stay ahead of the curve in that respect.

I am grateful for my life; I have worked hard for it. But it would certainly be wonderful to have a man to lean into. Just sayin'. Did you find any interesting meet-up groups?

Rats. I keep thinking today is Friday and it's not. Poop. Well, Edward, you have a great day, anyway ... Mindy

CHAPTER 5

MINDY:

When Edward and I speak tonight (Thursday), we agree we probably can never be the person each of us is looking for. I am touched by Edward's concern and dedication that I find a man logistically closer to me as he is attempting to find a woman closer to him. To this end, he contacts a couple of long-time friends from high school who live in my area to see if they know of anyone datable closer to my vicinity. I am at once pleased with the intention, and somewhat hopeful that this may be the way I actually meet my one true love. However.

The resulting consensus is that I will have a better chance of meeting someone if I learn to dance. Seriously?! I immediately get my snippy pants on and bemoan the fact that I have to change something about myself in order to appeal to a man. That this automatically means I am not good enough as I am. So I head down THAT path for awhile ... the ever popular "less than/woe is me" trek to a new bend in the road.

Happily, it doesn't last long as Edward's sincere desire to help outweighs my current bout of "what was I thinking?!"

> From: Edward
> To: Friends of Edward's
> Date: Thursday, July 28
> Subject: A Friend of Mine

Hey,
I have recently gone online in search of a lady friend. There are many lovely ladies in Richmond and around the DC

area. A few have made contact with me. They are cute and all, but too far away for me to consider on a practical level. I want a sweetie I can spend the night with and still get to work on time without a bunch of commuting trauma. Anyway, one of the ladies I have met lives in Reston. We have become friends. We know we won't itemize but we're buddies. I'm writing to ask if you know any eligible fellows worthy of sharing with my friend, Mindy. I'm attaching info about her to peruse yourself and to share if you know anyone. I know it's a long shot, but what the heck. I just upset Mindy because I've had 3 dates in 2 weeks, more than she's had in a year. It seems that all the folks you and I could fit with are almost always, way down the road. Not how it's supposed to be. Any assistance is appreciated. Hope things are well. Thank you.

Edward

From: Edward
To: Mindy
Date: Thursday, July 28
Subject: True Enlightenment

Hey Mindy, nice to hear from you bright and early. Glad the photo share worked. Yes, I am a lucky fellow. To have had hair and lost is better than to have never had hair at all. And I am lucky to have my son as well. I visited with him after work yesterday. We went to supper. Afterward, back at his place, he was speaking on the phone, I was watching and listening. I was pleasantly surprised to see and hear myself, a flashback to when I was his age (25 now). He was looking, speaking, sounding like me. I had never had that impression before. Way cool.

Girl, I feel your angst about standing in the hallway. I like that, the hallway addition to the open/closed window scenario. Sounds like something I could have made up. I've been lingering in the hall myself for awhile. You've got the right mindset, being an independent person so you have something to share besides need. But it becomes tedious and tiresome, waiting for the wheel to roll around to the sharing of a friend and lover.

I really understand wanting whomever to get on the stick, show up so you two can get on with things.

No special plans for the weekend. Try to get to the Y again to swim some more. There is always regular maintenance stuff to take care of. I am envious of your acupuncture therapy. I am blessed to be in good health. I have recently started taking care of checkup stuff that I should have done ten years ago. Found a personal doctor, got a good physical, had my first colonoscopy, yeehaa. All my results are good. Colonoscopy not nearly as traumatic as I was led to believe it would be.

We've had a busy, warm morning on the job, but now more action is calling so you and I will carry on later. Be good or ...
Edward

From: Mindy
To: Edward
Date: Thursday, July 28
Subject: RE: True Enlightenment

Hi Edward: I am sitting in a business meeting but wanted to say that your realization about your son looking, sounding, speaking like you is so very cool. I remember you mentioned it last night at the beginning of our conversation and I was so bent on yammering that I talked right over you. But I did hear you, and I apologize for tromping on your moment instead of asking to hear more about it, which, in hindsight, I really want to do. I am interested. It must be awesome to have a 25 year-old son who is finding his way. I am thinking he has a great dad so he will do just fine. When I think about some of the stuff I put my parents through I cringe. But it's all a part of finding out who we are, I guess.
Have a great rest of the day/evening.
Mindy

From: Edward
To: Mindy
Date: Friday, July 29
Subject: The Mindy Date Rodeo – Part 1

Good Morning Mindy,
I think I mentioned having friends who reside in Springfield, not so far from yourself. I asked if they might know any eligible gentlemen. Sadly that answer is a negatory. Gary suggested something silly; go learn how to dance the Carolina Shag. Sounds familiar to me, somehow. Oh yeah, I said that. I met a group of excellent folks. I also met two different ladies with whom there was sparkage. We quickly figured out that we weren't going to mesh for

doodah detail reasons but, we met, we tried. Anyway, point being, that avenue of action might work for you.

Down in this neck of the woods, sometime lessons are free, sometime there is a fee. Fees here are $7 - $10 per lesson. Either way, it's a worthy investment of time, energy and funds. And if you find that special fellow, it's priceless.

Attached is contact information for shag lessons in your area.

If you aren't interested in shag, go learn to salsa or something else. You need different action for different results. The more action, the more results, right? Well, it's supposed to work that way. The only certainty is that quitting is guaranteed failure and there's no fun or satisfaction in that. But you know these things.

I hope you have a good Friday. Try to pay attention in meetings, to the meetings. (I won't tell about your sideline activities.) I will forward the other mail right behind this. Edward

From: Mindy
To: Edward
Date: Friday, July 29
Subject: RE: The Mindy Date Rodeo – Part 1

Edward – OMG! This is great ... thanks so much for doing this work on my behalf. I will contact these folks straightaway! If I mention your name are they going to knock me to the floor and beat me senseless?? In any event, you are the best and I thank you for this ☺ and you are totally correct ... action follows action and energy creates energy ... law of physics. A body in motion keeps moving ... so ... get back Jack ... guess I am going to learn the shag. Whatever that is. Need to check out the YouTube videos. Step back and create a void for others to come in. I am working on creating the space in my life but also putting the energy out there to create the tracking beam to my heart (or...). You are a peach, my friend.

If you are around this weekend give me a yodel and we can chat. Have a great day. I am headed to my annual physical. Yep. Yeehaw! Also, as to your colonoscopy comment ... I find I look forward to them as it is the only time I get to ingest and enjoy druggage of the type they give prior to the procedure. These are the moments I live for. Well, not really. But it IS fun in a perverse sort of way.

Take care!

Mindy

From: Edward
To: Mindy
Date: Friday, July 29
Subject: Shake That Thang!

Hey Mindy,

Always glad to try to help a friend. The dance instructors up there don't have a clue who I am.

Interesting view of your colonoscopy. Almost sounds like you could take it up as a hobby, just for the good drugs, eh? I was expecting a reverse countdown when the drugs were administered. "We don't need no stinkin' countdown!" I went from awake to sleep with no warning. When I awakened, I couldn't tell you if anybody did anything. There were no marks or feelings of violation. There was a lot of internal air in need of being vented. It all worked out, pun intended. And I'm a healthy boy, yeah.

I want to send you an edition of the basic shag disc. Have I shared my address with you? If not, let me know and I will.

I'll let you get back to your day. Talk soon.

Edward

From: Edward
To: Mindy
Date: Friday, July 29
Subject: Fw: Fairfax County Shag Class – FALL
          Semester starts September 22

Hey Mindy

Here's more info about shag lessons, and most current. Impeccable timing. It is relephant (you know, the relephant in the room that nobody wants to talk about) to start lessons from the beginning. It's tough to start 2 or 3 weeks late. Like most things, each step/aspect builds on the previous. So your timing is great, you're early. The only thing better would be if classes started sooner but you will just have to be brave. In the mean time you can learn the basic with the Carolina Shag DVD that I will send you. Go Girl!

Edward

CHAPTER 6

From: ClarityNow
To: FunMrEdward
Date: Friday, July 29
Subject: Are you working today ...

... or just being my social secretary??? If I learn to dance will you dance with me? Just got into work so I need to be serious for a bit. But only a bit. Thanks for all the info ... that is FAB, my friend. And so appreciated. Do you want to talk via phone at some point this weekend? And, yes, you have my address right. Thanks again! Mindy

From: FunMrEdward
To: ClarityNow
Date: Friday, July 29
Subject: Re: Are you working today ...

I'm doing both, working and being Secretariat ... huh? Nothing equine here. We are bravely standing by, ready to leap into action at a moment's notice. Four trucks scheduled for the day but have not seen any yet. They'll show up at 3. We get off at 4. However, it will be fine.
I will dance with you even if you don't learn how. Admittedly, it will go more smoothly if you learn, but either way, I'm in.

Noticed that you caught and enjoyed The Meaning Of Life on my FB page. I liked that muchly myself. It was shared by a music friend at the beach.

Share a couple of windows of opportunity for your

availability and I will call you this weekend. I would like that. Be as serious as is appropriate. Soon speak.
Edward

From: Mindy
To: Edward
Date: Friday, July 29
Subject: Edward!!

Dude, I have to leave tomorrow (Saturday) to go into DC around noon. Are you available to chat before then? I am thinking it is easier to touch base earlier rather than later since you seem to have a never-ending number of dates traipsing through your life. ☺

This is a particularly busy weekend for me (when I would much rather be lollygagging and not running willy-nilly) but it is what it is. It's all good stuff. Let me know what works for you.

It would be great to hear your voice ...
Mindy

From: Edward
To: Mindy
Date: Saturday, July 30
Subject: Manana

Hey Mindy,
You said you wanted to speak some more so I will call you manana. What time frame works for you? Share a clue, please. Looking forward. ... Edward

From: Mindy
To: Edward
Date: Saturday, July 30
Subject: RE: Manana

Hi Edward,

How about later tonight? Just got back from my marathon acupuncture session ... SO interesting. I have about a million more sessions to go ... I am expecting GREAT things. ☺ Are you around later tonight? I have a meeting tomorrow morning and then company picnic from 1-5. After that I have to write a contract for early Monday. Blah, blah, blah. I need to jump in the shower and get this oil off me. ☺ Anyway ... I know you have a life so if you aren't available to speak tonight I totally get that.

  Let me know your thoughts. I am thinking you would like to chat more, too, but that may be a grandiose assumption on my part. Dude.

Peace out,
Mindy

From: Mindy
To: Edward
Date: Saturday, July 30
Subject: RE: Manana revisited

Okay, tomorrow (Sunday) it is ... 8:30? I need to leave the house about 9:40am so we can have our coffee together prior to that? I get home from the meeting about 11:30 and don't have to leave again until 1pm (for the company picnic) this weekend is a tad more time/engagement intensive than most.

Hope you're out having an ab-fab dating experience of some sort ... you deserve it ... of course I will be totally jealous but since I am living vicariously through you make it a good one. ;-)

Talk soon,

Mindy

From:	ClarityNow
To:	FunMrEdward
Date:	Sunday, July 31
Subject:	Profile change

In keeping with the ever-demanding pastime of profile fine-tuning I have added non-smokers (the only way I would be able to kiss someone for days) and cowboy boots. So far, I haven't been hit up for any bus tickets (shades of Midnight Cowboy).

Hope you had a great rest of the day. So enjoyed our earlier chat(s), both online and off. Talk soon,

Mindy

MINDY:

A Word About Online Profile Photos

True, I am a neophyte when it comes to online profiles but ... really ... who thinks it is a good idea for a man to pose with a dead fish? The only thing I can figure out is that it is proof of being a good provider. Or maybe a subtle hint as to, "this is what I will be doing every weekend" and/or "you are going to be cleaning these bad boys." Better a fish than a dead deer carcass. Or a Corvette. There seems to be a lot of grandstanding around those, too.

It is something of the adult version of "show and tell." I find it intriguing that so many folks show and tell the same things. It makes me wonder if they do any research prior to posting their profile online.

Not that I haven't been ridiculed for some of my photos. Payback is a bitch.

From: FunMrEdward
To: ClarityNow
Date: Sunday, July 31
Subject: Re: Profile change

Hey Girl,
Just finished supper and came up to see what condition our condition was in. And here you are!
Changing your profile filters can certainly provide different results. More or less, depending which way you go. Nixing smokers reduces the crowd but enhances the pleasure of your experience. I was originally a social smoker but have become a non-smoker. Phew, slid under your radar on that one. It would be yummy to explore kissing for days ... Now cowboy boots, I haven't owned a pair of those since I was eight. Better tighten up my act, eh? My moccasin boots died a couple weeks ago. Darn. Meet you barefoot, on gentle ground.
I too enjoyed our conversations today. Soon speak.
Edward

CHAPTER 7

MINDY:

Edward mentions the possibility of coming to my neck of the woods to visit his long-time friends, who also share his love of motorcycles. To that end, we begin to talk about our "bus station" meeting, even though we really have no plans to do so at this time. It is fun to put the intention out there; a bit like sticking my toe into suggestive waters to see if Edward is amenable to an innocent meeting at some point. He is.

From:	ClarityNow
To:	FunMrEdward
Date:	Sunday, July 31
Subject:	I will totally…

… pick you up at the bus depot. I have no idea where it is but I have Mapquest and I know how to use it. :-) Have you actually become a non-smoker or did you just put that in your profile to get more kissable women to respond? I have to admit that is definitely something I look for. I figure that folks tell you about 10% of the truth when it comes to such things. There is a big difference between smoking the occasional cigar around a bonfire with the guys and needing to light up a cig at every opportunity. And, for some reason I can't explain, I love cowboy boots … perhaps I was Annie Oakley in another life … however, it is not a prerequisite … although I have had a couple of guys respond in direct reference to the boot addition to my profile. Of course, both of them are shorter than me so not the effect I was looking for. :-(Then again, as we have discussed, it is all about fine-tuning and getting the message out there so the universe can work on things.

I admire your intention to put things in order. I believe you are a very good man, Mr. Fun Edward. :-) Now get that second part-time job at 7-11 and hop on that bus! I can say these things because I, too, have been trying to scrap together some sort of retirement plan. If I had known I was going to live this long, I would have paid more attention to what I was doing. It's all good. Take care, my friend, and talk soon.

Mindy

From: FunMrEdward
To: ClarityNow
Date: Sunday, July 31
Subject: Glowing Profiles at the Bus Station

Hey Mindy,

I will have to go visit your new revised profile and check on the boot situation. Those fellows, who responded, suggest that they get boots with heels high enough to at least match your height. Are they close enough to think about? And to reiterate what I said earlier, if you see a face and/or soul that catches your eye/spirit, reach out, say hello. There doesn't seem to be a success pattern based on who reached out first, so go for it. "Hi, I'm Mindy and I like the look of your stuff and the way you talk about it… What's up, whatchu wanna do?" Get down with your good/bad self girl. Don't miss an opportunity to say "hello." We never know how it will turn out.

Thank you for your nice words about trying to take care of stuff. It's all selfish on my part. Taking care of crap is easier than not taking care of it, and then it turns into more/bigger crap. As I can, I try to make the pile of stuff smaller, if possible.

So, I will totally be waiting for you at the bus station, you smart, cute sassy girl. Soon speak.
Edward

From:	ClarityNow
To:	FunMrEdward
Date:	Sunday, July 31
Subject:	Re: Glowing Profiles at the Bus Station

Edward, you are TOO funny! And don't worry, I am not hanging my heart on our bus stop meeting, although it would be easy to do … but not fair to put that kind of pressure on either one of us. So, yes, I am smiling (however you do that online) and playing nice with the boys and not being horrified at some of the come-ons … the good news is that I am regaining (if I ever had it to begin with) some semblance of similar comeonage (new made up word!) and see where that goes. Some are in this area. The ones that are too far away … like several time zones … I am cutting loose with a kind word. No true connection and I am not into double-wides … in any sense of the word. I am always polite. I learned that from you. And, truth be told, I would MUCH rather meet YOU at a bus depot than talk to men who HAVE to wear cowboy boots in order to reach the pedals. So … there you have it. Putting the best energy forward that I can muster. Still standing in the hallway but happy that you are here with me. Sweet dreams ... Mindy

The Dating Site - Online chat
Date: Monday, August 1
<u>Claritynow:</u> Hey, chatty boy. ☺

<u>FunMrEdward:</u> Hey girl, how's by you?

<u>Claritynow:</u> Just got back from yoga.

<u>FunMrEdward:</u> Good deal, stretching them parts, keep the blood and juices flowing freely.

<u>Claritynow:</u> Yep ... surely would be nice to have someone else to focus on other than me.

<u>FunMrEdward:</u> Keep beating them bushes.

<u>Claritynow:</u> lol ... indeed.

<u>Claritynow:</u> I now have a throng of tiny men in cowboy boots.

<u>FunMrEdward:</u> I was just looking back to see which of us instigated this thing we got going on, it was you, long about July 21st. // LOL, a throng of tiny men in cowboy boots, eh. Did you specify tiny men?

Claritynow: No ... just the cowboy boots ... I need to re-think my profile again ... more fine-tuning. Wow! Seems like we have been talking for ages ... 7/21?

FunMrEdward: Do you have a Frank Zappa connection? He seemed to have an affinity for tiny things, in his songs. That's the date on the mail of me responding to your first message. Yes, my friend, it seems longer than that, which is not a bad thing.

Claritynow: Nope ... not a bad thing at all ... and no connection to Zappa ... I will be sad when you run off with some sweet young thang. But maybe she'll have a brother and we can double date ... wouldn't THAT be way weird.

FunMrEdward: That could be a hoot. I have wanted to have friends for me and my lady to play with. That could work out.

Claritynow: I like the baggage quote ... about someone loving you enough to help you unpack ... nice.

FunMrEdward: Thought you would like that.

FunMrEdward: Say, do you have any regard for astrology?

Claritynow: In what way?

FunMrEdward: I find it interesting how accurate many of the observations are. I found a site that I use to check compatibilities and I was going to share the address if you care. This is also a good sidestep from the group grope comment above.

Claritynow: I totally missed the group grope comment. I am entirely too innocent for the likes of you. ☺ Or so it would seem.

FunMrEdward: Yes, a lovely innocent with a heart and parts that all deserve considerable love and attention.

Claritynow: Now that is putting it mildly ... I am sitting here reading the e-mail you sent earlier ... I love that you are intent on finding me a man.

Claritynow: And I do track certain folks in saved files so I don't get confused ... I don't have the bandwidth to keep track of too many at any given time ... and for some reason it seems a bit tawdry to have all of these score cards. So I try to keep current. You are my current current.

FunMrEdward: I told you, if it's not me, I'm glad to try and help. Are you up for motorcycling?

Claritynow: Yes.

FunMrEdward: Good on motorcycling. I am complimented to be your current currant, so to speak.

Claritynow: Not that there is anything raisin-y about you ... aren't currants raisins?

Claritynow: I have a couple of other irons in the fire, so to speak, but they live further away than you do. What is up with THAT?

FunMrEdward: Yes ma'am. Farther is the wrong direction, but you know that. Who reached out? Can they travel? Folks who are free of the job doodah restraints can be viable candidates.

Claritynow: True dat. But I still work ... there lies the rub.

FunMrEdward: But if they don't, they can come see you.

Claritynow: Yes. One of these days I will tell you my brilliant plan for the next step in my life ... should no one step INTO my life before I decide to move on.

FunMrEdward: Are you in need of urging? Where are you moving on to?

Claritynow: Not sure of where but am getting clearer on the "what" ... but that is subject to change if someone comes calling. I am just trying to stay open and keep the space clear for a man to come in ... but, given my propensity for planning I do like to have a Plan B in case I continue solo on this journey. Which would suck but you never know how things are going to turn out. Not to get all maudlin ...

FunMrEdward: I must say, a plan of "what" that doesn't have room for a friend does not come to mind, other than becoming a nun. And where's the fun in that?

Claritynow: No ... I meant that my plan def includes someone else BUT if they don't show up then I can do it myself. However, if (when) someone shows up then there is all the fun of planning things together ... which is beyond exciting to me. Amongst other things ...

FunMrEdward: Okay, I understand now. Having a plan B is excellent. I don't. I have aspirations but not a plan. Need to work on that, seriously. Finding that friend would help the development of a plan, but you so smart, to be working on the potentially solo plan. I need to tighten up.

Claritynow: It's just the way I was raised. The importance of being able to take care of yourself. I come from a family of brothers so probably got the message via osmosis. Although my dad always said it was important to make my own way and not rely on others.

Claritynow: Plans are infinitely more fun to do with someone you plan on spending your life with. A plan can mean nothing more than living on the beach and being present for someone you love, every day.

FunMrEdward: Yes ma'am, they certainly are. Well, I've always been independent and self-sufficient. I guess

I have the resources. You seem to have a beach fetish. Being present for someone you love is why we are here, on this site, on this earth. It's just finding the beggars, right?

Claritynow: Yes. The beach fetish is because it was my happiest time. Newly sober in a place of great beauty and calm. And salt water/air is so healing for the system. So, as one ages, it would make sense to settle in an environment that would be physically supportive. Throw in a happening relationship and that is about as good as it gets. However, I am pretty much open to anywhere … but no place with dreary weather.

FunMrEdward: That is as good as it gets. So there's no going back to the Northwest permanently.

Claritynow: No. I only go there in the summer.

Claritynow: I could be bi-coastal. ☺

Claritynow: I would like to meet you.

FunMrEdward: An AC/DC kind of existence. When are you going back for dad's 90th birthday?

Claritynow: August 20 – Sept 3.

FunMrEdward: I don't think I'll be up your way in that time frame. I'll try to not plan it for then. Does bicoastal mean you have to dress up in exotic clothing?

Claritynow: Not necessarily.

FunMrEdward: You slipped that "want to meet me" thing in and it took me a moment to pick up on that. I would be hurt if you felt otherwise. Meeting and sharing our faces is part of our short term desire and plan. In my agenda, anyway. No doubt. Just when is the question. Next couple of months is the answer. Not quickly enough but it beats a blank.

Claritynow: Thank you for saying that.

FunMrEdward: Only truth.

Claritynow: My thought is that I so enjoy our chats and it would be very cool to just sit and have a nice long conversation about all of this … yes, always only truth … I can't do it any other way and I know you are like that, too, which is beyond amazing.

FunMrEdward: And be able to hold hands or cuddle while we do. Yes'm.

Claritynow: Two months of this and it is possible we will just burn ourselves out and miss it entirely … def to the holding/cuddling thing.

FunMrEdward: LOL … I've typed my heart out and my fingers down to nubs and I can't take it anymore. As Pete Townsend (Who) said, "I've got blisters on me fingers."

Claritynow: Are you tired of typing tonight? Sorry to do this so late in the evening. Damn yoga.

FunMrEdward: Good yoga. I'm not tired of typing but it is past my bedtime so I should be going. There is more keyboard left. We don't have to use it up at one time.

FunMrEdward: Good yoga, keep your butt cute, right?

Claritynow: That's the plan. Sweet dreams, my friend.

FunMrEdward: Sweet dreams, lady. Good night.

.

CHAPTER 8

From: FunMrEdward
To: ClarityNow
Date: Monday, August 1
Subject: Faked me out

Once again, I stumble across your porch light burning only to find that I am a moth, but you aren't answering the door. But that's alright. I like standing here in the hallway with you. Wish we could hold hands. Looking forward to sharing the beach. In the meantime, sweet dreams lady.

From: ClarityNow
To: FunMrEdward
Date: Tuesday, August 2
Subject: Re: Faked me out

Good morning, Mr. Fun! I saw that you were online last night but fought the inclination to stalk you for the third time in one day. ☺ Plus, if we started chatting I would never get to bed cuz I would much rather hang with you than be responsible, get to bed early only to wake up at this ungodly hour AND gird my loins (do women do that??) for the client meeting at 10am. I would much rather put on my Pollyanna duds and skip on down to the beach. So take my hand and let's def do it, my friend.
Mindy

From: FunMrEdward
To: ClarityNow
Date: Monday, August 1
Subject: Re: Faked Me Out ... No, You Faked Me Out

Yes, you faked me out. But that was good. You are right about being up way too late. It was your turn to be the grown up and you did it well.

Heck of a time to be up 4:35. Of course, my alarm goes off twenty minutes later. But that's a personal problem.

Yes, it is appropriate for women to gird their loins, literally and figuratively. (Maybe we could make our fortune by opening a string of gird shops. I'm a little sketchy on where to find a supplier.)

Please don't think me rude or ugly but I hope you didn't pay good money for the whole ... "it is what it is" ... thing. That statement does not answer the question of what something is. And of course, everything is what it is. Question is, what the heck is it? A simple direct answer will do, please. No cosmic karmic non-answering BS, psycho-emotional doodah kind of stuff. But that's just me.

Regardless of what you are wearing, I will hold your hand and go to the beach, or elsewhere. Until then, be good.
Edward

From: ClarityNow
To: FunMrEdward
Date: Monday, August 1
Subject: Stalking ...

... yep ... it's me again ...

From: FunMrEdward
To: ClarityNow
Date: Monday, August 1
Subject: Re: Stalking ...

There you go, wearing your stockings again, but you don't tell me about them or show them to me. That's just not right. If you are going to toy with my emotions, at least do it in a complete format. Please.

From: FunMrEdward
To: ClarityNow
Date: Monday, August 1
Subject: Re: Stalking ...

LOL ... you are such a goose ... but cuter than cute so completely forgivable. Dude, what up?

From: FunMrEdward
To: ClarityNow
Date: Monday, August 1
Subject: What Up ...

Hey girl,
"Everybody has baggage. It's all about finding the one who loves you enough to help you unpack."
  I thought that was pretty cool. Also, astute.
  The upside, or downside to revisiting profiles online is that

the observee can tell that you were back. Sometimes you might want a refresher without appearing to be stalking someone. But if you want them to know you're interested, cut through the mystery and reach out. It's easy to be bold from behind the keyboard. You just need to be that person/presence in three dimensions. Don't make promises we can't keep.

I've noticed that this venue is like having purchased a Lotto ticket that could pay off at any moment. Each visit back has an air of anticipation. Who's come calling, will I care, and is it my grandmother/father looking to hook up? Will they be literate? Will it be someone who will help me unpack? An interesting little roller coaster event. What do you think?

You did tell me you liked motorcycles. You could wear your cowgirl boots.

I need to get back to being responsible. Oh, I mailed your shag DVD today. It should be there in a couple days. I hope you enjoy. It will give you a leg up when you get to classes. Go girl.

Talk soon. Edward

From: FunMrEdward
To: ClarityNow
Date: Tuesday, August 2
Subject: Re: What up? ... We up!

We've had an action-packed, fun-filled day over here on the job, and there's good chance of some more before we go home. Temp is only 95, so we just sweat instead of steep.

Good for my weight loss program, though. Closer to my girlish figure.

I really should be in bed with the lights out at 9 but somehow I never make it before 10. How adult is that? But I enjoyed our visit last night. So, not to worry. If you see my porch light on, say howdy, please, if you are inclined.
Catch you later.
Edward

From: FunMrEdward
To: ClarityNow
Date: Tuesday, August 2
Subject: Re: What up? ... We up!

Hey Sweetie, we were busy all day on the job. I got your message and started to respond and we got called out immediately. I've been snooping around here for a few minutes, saw you online and tried to touch base. You seemed to be busy, so I hope it is with a possible Mr. Wonderful. Cowboy boots and not tiny. Get down with your good/bad sweet self. Let me know how it worked out. Bedtime lady. Hit me back tomorrow. Sweet dreams.
Edward

From: ClarityNow
To: FunMrEdward
Date: Friday, August 5
Subject: Friday night ...

... I'm thinking you have a hot date ... tru dat? If so, good for you, my friend. :-) I am lying low ... long week and happy to have a couple of days off. Talk soon, Mindy

From: FunMrEdward
To: ClarityNow
Date: Saturday, August 6
Subject: Saturday morning

Good morning Mindy,
Last night I went to Norfolk and visited with my son. I understand the long week/lay low theory and reality. I'm looking forward to visiting today, but also looking forward to low laying tomorrow. Get some rest girl. Get prepared for the next whatever. Hope you got a cowboy headed your way. Take care. Soon speak.
Edward

From: ClarityNow
To: FunMrEdward
Date: Saturday, August 6
Subject: Re: Saturday morning

Hi Edward ... nice that you are spending time with your son. Priceless, actually. I am heading into DC for the afternoon. Will be around tomorrow. Hope your date goes great! Keeping my fingers crossed for you ... does she live close by? Just be your adorable self. Talk soon, my friend. Mindy

From: ClarityNow
To: FunMrEdward
Date: Sunday, August 7
Subject: Edward!!!

Dude ... we are like two ships passing in the night ... however, it sounds like you are having QUITE the weekend, my friend. :-) Hope so, anyway. I was in DC when you called. I am now heading to a hair appointment cuz it is NOT easy maintaining this level of cuteness on personality alone. Then a late lunch/early din with a friend. Wow. Just typing this makes me want to take a nap ... talk soon ... Mindy

From: ClarityNow
To: FunMrEdward
Date: Sunday, August 7
Subject: Sorry I missed your call ...

... it's getting late so don't want to open the chat window as that will just get me chatty and I'm trying to settle in for bed. It's all about me. :-) So happy you had a full weekend and are making new friends. How could you not? You are a wonderful man and I envy the woman that gets you for keeps. Talk soon,
Mindy

CHAPTER 9

EDWARD:

While speaking with Mindy, we discuss some of the messages we are getting on the site, especially the Flirts from people without pictures. One of the Flirts is "Tell me about your profile picture." This is the perfect response to the faceless people and I started sending it back to them. Mindy finds this strategy helpful and humorous.

From:	ClarityNow
To:	FunMrEdward
Date:	Monday, August 8
Subject:	So happy ...

... you told me about the Flirt message for the folks who don't have a photo ... perfect! How was your day? Mindy

From:	FunMrEdward
To:	ClarityNow
Date:	Monday, August 8
Subject:	Re: So happy ...

Go Girl,

I got a good giggle out of that. Hoping to speak with the other new online acquaintance this evening. Not sure of her schedule so I asked that she call me. Will see how that goes.

How was your day? Hope well.

Be good. Edward

From: ClarityNow
To: FunMrEdward
Date: Tuesday, August 9
Subject: Re: So happy ...

Morning, Edward ... be careful that you don't waste away to nothing ...   :-)   I am 5'6" and vacillate (for years now) between 127-130. I need to work more on muscle tone than losing weight. I have such a sedentary job ... when I'm not running willy-nilly to clients' appointments, in which case I am sitting behind a steering wheel. I have been a total slacker about going to the gym. And then there is the whole gravity thing. WTF?!

I am utilizing your brilliant idea of sending Flirts to folks who have no profile, no picture, and, apparently, no command of the English language. At least I don't feel like I am totally dissing them ... but what is it about me and my people-pleasing ways that makes me feel like I am responsible for other people's (complete strangers!) feelings? It reminds me of the line from "Alice in Wonderland"- "Move down, clean cups!" I am moving my way through the throngs (well, that might be a gross overstatement) of curious males on this site at a break neck pace!

Time to get ready for work. Be careful out there in the heat ... have an ab-fab day. Happy that you are meeting some interesting women of substance. You deserve someone as wonderful as you. Talk soon,
Mindy

From: Mindy
To: Edward
Date: Wednesday, August 10
Subject: Shag!

Edward ☺
Just signed up for my dance classes … Yeehaw … they start 9/22…
Later, gator … Mindy

From: ClarityNow
To: FunMrEdward
Date: Wednesday, August 10
Subject: Apology

Dear Edward, in an earlier e-mail I made light of the fact that you were thinking of dating someone who may have health issues. In hindsight (about 5 minutes ago … that is how slow I am) I remember that you took care of your wife and her health issues for many years. I sincerely apologize for my lack of sensitivity.

  I hope you had a good day at work. It was less humid here so hoping the same for you. Talk soon, Mindy

From: FunMrEdward
To: ClarityNow
Date: Wednesday, August 10
Subject: Re: Apology

Dear Mindy,

There is no need to apologize for anything. You were not insensitive about a thing. I brought it up. Health issues are one of the things I had momentarily overlooked (mental checklist of desirable qualities in a partner). We need to maintain the awareness of the important, non-negotiable parts of our partner list of qualities.

CHAPTER 10

From: Mindy
To: Edward
Date: Thursday, August 11
Subject: How far are you from ...

... Bethany Beach? Probably a million miles but just thought I would ask.
Peace out.
Mindy

From: Edward
To: Mindy
Date: Thursday, August 11
Subject: Re: How far are you from ...

The electron map says 181 miles, 3 hours and 47 minutes. Why do you ask? You got some hot picnic action? Oh, it's in Delaware. I looked in VA but the map knew better, fortunately. Hit me back.
Edward

From: Mindy
To: Edward
Date: Thursday, August 11
Subject: RE: How far are you from ...

A friend is renting a beach house in mid-September and I am going to be there for the weekend ... I think the 17th

& 18th ... ??? Dunno ... just a thought ... I hadn't looked at a map when I asked you. By then you will probably be married ☺

MINDY:

Every summer, a friend of mine rents a house at Bethany Beach for a week. This year she has invited me to join her and a couple of her women friends. The thought occurs to me that this would be a great time to actually meet Edward, face to face. In my geographical ineptitude, I assume that if there is a beach involved it must be pretty close to his home, which is somewhere in the vicinity of Norfolk. Silly me. Bethany is farther for him to travel than it is for me. Rats.

At this point in my part of the story, I need to clarify with Edward regarding our conversations and intention. It is heady stuff. We talk of meeting with the realization that it is a casual meeting. Mutual curiosity and verbal attraction. We have talked at length about such things; fun, flirty chats tinged in hope and longing (at least on my part ... I'm still not sure about Edward's but I have great hopes and he seems totally transparent in his objectives.) He is completely forthcoming about his past, the fact that he is a widower and has an adult son, and is trying, at this late point in his life, striving to pull a pension together for retirement. A background check proves this all to be true (I'm not an idiot!). His honesty floors me.

EDWARD:

So, on Thursday, Mindy had the idea of us meeting in person and she blurted it out, on paper, on the electron screen, but most definitely blurted. She and I have been talking for three weeks. Heck, after three days it was as if we had known each other for years. We discussed everything from the highly abstract to the totally intimate. We were both interested in sex and not shy about saying so. We were not lascivious, just honest. Sex is not the only nice thing for women and men to share, but it's one of the most pleasant. It *is* if you are doing it well, anyway ... and with the right person.

Poor girl, she told me she had not had sex with anyone but herself for seven years. Self-sufficiency is great and useful, but that's a long time to not have a sweetheart to share with. It had been a year for me, and that was a year longer than I wanted it to be that way. But it is amazing what folks can do without, how they can get along despite hardships (or lack of hard-ships, as the case may be).

In one of our earliest conversations, Mindy had commented that she wanted to have sex with another person, at least once more before she died. I certainly could sympathize and concur. I had not a clue that it might work out for her to share that experience with me. Remember, we were just being supportive buddies.

From: Edward
To: Mindy
Date: Friday, August 12
Subject: RE: How far are you from ...

Good Morning Mindy,
Is this a tentative invitation to come up and visit? My world is still in flux. I haven't any idea when the bike ride weekend will come together. A plan to visit could

71

be made. Is it better to visit away from home, or just different? Is it a visit with your friend weekend, or an available place without friend emphasis? Questions, questions. Oh bother. No brides on my horizon that I know of.

Take care, girl.

Edward

From: Mindy
To: Edward
Date: Friday, August 12
Subject: RE: How far are you from ...

"I'm curious about your thoughts, young lady, about Bethany Beach."

Dear Edward,

Yes, I am curious about that, as well. I think you are going out tonight? If not, give me a yodel and we can chat about it. Have a good rest of the day. I signed a new project this morning so am feeling good about that. It's all grist for the mill. This weather is beyond amazing ... totally makes me want to play.

Talk soon,

Mindy

MINDY:

Edward always wears his blue tooth when we talk and is able to multi-task during our marathon phone conversations.

He is a very busy and organized person. Focused in a scattershot sort of way. I, on the other, hand languish on the chaise and just focus on his amazing voice and intriguing insights. I revel in the thrill of his attention. I am starved for it. I feel like I am 40 years younger. It is amazing.

One of the things I notice is that time is not linear for Edward. It has taken me quite a few, "when did that happen?" interjections into his stories for me to realize that when he says "a couple of weeks ago" he is referring to an incident that took place somewhere in the 1970's. I tend to be more literal, and catch myself asking for clarification.

I believe that this nailing down of facts is also my way of making sure that what I am sensing about Edward is true. That he is who he says he is and not some whacko in hiding … just waiting for the opportune moment to tromp on my heart. Even though, of course, our hearts can never truly commingle due to distance and whatever else we have thrown up between us. It is scary to be so happy.

From:	Edward
To:	Mindy
Date:	Friday, August 12
Subject:	How Close Are We To Bethany Beach?

Dear Mindy,
Yes ma'am, I am going out tonight. Time and space is such that I need to move on along, no real free time.

I want to yodel with you about Bethany Beach (as soon as possible, inquiring minds want to know) but I do not want to be rushed when we discuss it. I enjoy our idyllic time spent on the phone. What if you call me after you get home from work tomorrow, or tell me what time you'll be available and I can call you. Does one of those sound alright? I'd like to be curious with you.

I'm sorry you have to work tomorrow. Sometimes we just have to buck up.

Yes, you did share your cell number, than kew vury mush. Have a good afternoon and evening my friend. I anticipate your reply about yodeling time, with worms in my mouth, otherwise known as baited breath (thank you for that observation, Robin Williams).

Soon speak. Edward

From: Mindy
To: Edward
Date: Friday, August 12
Subject: RE: How Close Are We To Bethany Beach?

Dear Edward,

Have a great time tonight. Perhaps you'll fall in love ... or lust ... or just have a fun time, in general. You deserve it.

Yes, we need time to explore the Bethany Beach idea. It popped into my head and I blurted it out. Apparently, you are an easy man to blurt things out to. Definitely a nice long chat is in order. I very much enjoy when we are able to do that. I will call you tomorrow early evening? Not sure how I will be when I get home from doing the talky-talk with the crowd. It tuckers me out sometimes. So it will probably be between 4-6pm? Does that work for you? I have no plans for tomorrow evening except pre-emptive packing for my trip out west. You are the one with a social

life so you tell me what works.
Break a leg ;-)
Mind

From: Edward
To: Mindy
Date: Friday, August 12
Subject: Subject: Re: How Close Are We To Bethany
Beach?

Dear Mindy,
Tonight's visit is with Date #3, the lady from last Saturday. At the moment I'm falling in friendship, and that is fine. I hope to fall into more and I'm not sure it will happen with her, but that's alright also. I am not ready to close my eyes to other possibilities. With her, I will have at least found a friend, perhaps more.

My tomorrow is free form so you calling between 4 and 6 sounds excellent. I'm glad the idea popped and you blurted. We will discuss, like responsible adults (who is this guy trying to fool?), right? Sure.

Good you have a plan. I trust you can bring it together, for your own benefit. Making that space for a lucky man, mmmm.

Time to pack it up here and head into the evening. Thanks for the rapid response and the contact plan. I'm looking forward to our chat. Have a good evening and manana.
Edward

CHAPTER 11

MINDY:

Once we realize how far the mutual trip to Bethany Beach would be, Edward and I decide instead to meet halfway between our homes. We pick a spot on the map. This involves a 1.5 hour drive for each of us, on I-95 (north and south, respectively.)

This mid-point is a small college town called Ashland. Lucky them. I am thinking a college town is going to be more amenable to our meeting. Not sure why. This is beginning to feel more and more like 1970. Not a bad thing.

From: Edward
To: Mindy
Date: Saturday, August 13
Subject: Halfway to Nirvana

Dear Mindy Girl,
I decided not to go shagging tonight. Need to finish cleaning my room (go clean your room young man!).

On to pleasantness: The center of Ashland is two miles beyond halfway for you. That means we need to camp just north of town for it to be halfway. What do you think? Have you got a pup tent? Maybe I can borrow one. Well, I like hot and cold running toilets so, what if I book us a room in, or around Ashland? Meet Sunday, September 4th, knock around town, have a pajama party and go home Monday afternoon. Does that work for you? I hope so.

I just checked hotels and found the Overnight Suites, with a King Suite. King size bed, sofa if you kick me out, fridge and microwave. There is a pool (no idea what size) and an exercise room. Breakfast included. Non-smoking, of course. What you think girl? Shall I book us?

I'm as excited as a school girl ... something like that.
Edward

From: Mindy
To: Edward
Date: Saturday, August 13
Subject: RE: Halfway to Nirvana

Dear Edward,
I'm in. AND I can't believe I am doing this ... however, feels good doing it with you ☺ At least I'm pretty sure that will be the case ...

Will you send me the hotel link for a visual ... sounds perfecto ... ?
Talk soon, Mindy

From: Edward
To: Mindy
Date: Saturday, August 13
Subject: Re: PS.

Hooray for us! I will go ahead and book up.

EDWARD:

So now, this lovely young woman, who lives too far away and is not the right woman for the rest of my life, with whom I get along and carry on so freely and comfortably, but has invited me to meet her half way, and perhaps, all the way. We talked about getting a suite with a bed and a sofa bed so we do not have to sleep together. I assure her that I am a gentleman and capable of sleeping in the same room with her, and sleeping only. I can do it. I know I can, I know I can. It could turn out that we do not like each other after all, despite our many pleasant phone conversations. Or, we could meet and share our bodies as intimately as we have shared our minds and spirits. Oh, what's a boy to do? Be brave young man, be brave. How much we will share is still an unknown. But discovering the unknown is part and parcel of us meeting in person anyway.

From: Edward
To: Mindy
Date: Saturday, August 13
Subject: Hurray!!

Dear Ms. Mindy,
I just made the reservation and you should have received confirmation. I am not sure you can get to the hotel info from that, so here is the address that I am looking at.

I checked out the "Things To Do" tab. Also checked on restaurants. The photo of the front of the hotel looks like a flat facade, a movie prop (right end of building makes me see that). I hope the building has that third dimension that I'm not seeing in the photo. Otherwise, we're going to be a bit cramped. What does your constructing eye see?

Get down with your sweet/bad self, girl. I can hardly contain myself. Good thing this body is self contained.

Oh excellent! Edward

From: Edward
To: Mindy
Date: Saturday, August 13
Subject: PS

Oops, I meant to add; Erase the pencil, and with the pen I write "Mindy" on my calendar. Oh excellent!

From: Mindy
To: Edward
Date: Saturday, August 13
Subject: Lordy

Dear Edward,
You're right ... we have apparently booked a hotel room located on some abandoned Hollywood film lot. At least it's not the Bates Hotel ... that would be setting the limbo bar pretty alarmingly low. Actually, the room looks nice. Do you think we should book two in case we don't even LIKE each other??

   I am sitting here (sitting being the operative word) wondering how I am going to get cute in only three weeks time. Unlike you, I have not been working out or hoisting 22 lb chains around every day. Just sayin ...
I am beyond excited. Lordy.
Whew ☺
Mindy

From: Edward
To: Mindy

Date: Saturday, August 13
Subject: RE: Lordy

Dear Mindy,
We already know that we don't "not like" each other. If we don't want to sleep together, I will sleep on the sofa. If we do sleep together, I am capable of just sleeping, if necessary. We will figure out how much we want to share, and it will be good and fine and wonderful.

   The fact that you are aware and interested in your cutitude is the key. You just have to do something regularly to make stuff better. That being said, bring your cute self on over to meet me, girl and it will be fine. That kind of change takes time so don't sweat it (is that pun intended or pun not intended, I'm not sure), don't be concerned about that, okay?

   So, to borrow from a friend, "I am beyond excited. Lordy. Whew ☺"

From: Mindy
To: Edward
Date: Saturday, August 13
Subject: RE: Lordy

Dear Edward,
Thank you for that. You take the edge off my "what ifs" ☺
Time to head to bed. Tomorrow I have my 10 am meeting and then go into DC for acupuncture with the Sufi.
Sweet dreams!
Mindy

From: Edward
To: Mindy
Date: Saturday, August 13
Subject: RE: Lordy

Dear Mindy,
Our sharing is our pleasure. It has been so and will continue to be. It is mutual, respect, admiration, appreciation, desire, curiosity, and a whole bunch more I'm sure. So it will be wondermous. Sweetheart, yes, pleased and excited. Worms in my mouth.

  Yes, it is past both our bedtimes. Hope your acupuncture hits the spot.

  Sweet dreams, dear.

  Edward

CHAPTER 12

From: Mindy
To: Edward
Date: Sunday, August 14
Subject: RE: Lordy

Dear Edward,
A good night's sleep and woke up still thinking this is still the BEST IDEA EVER ... just sayin ... Heading into DC ... Talk soon, Mindy

From: Edward
To: Mindy
Date: Sunday, August 14
Subject: RE: Lordy

Dear Mindy,
I'm just saying, I'm glad you feel the same after a good night's sleep. The BEST IDEA EVER! I'm pleased you don't have planner's remorse. It will continue to be the BEST IDEA EVER! I am stoked (how long has it been since you heard, or I used that term?).
   I'm headed to the Y to swim some laps. Hope your day is swell.
Soon speak. Edward

From: Edward
To: Mindy
Date: Sunday, August 14

Subject: RE: Deal Breakers

Hey Girl,
Just got home a few minutes ago (23:00) and wanted to
see about your stoked self, indeed, my stoked self, indeed!
   And so my dear friend, I trust you are already asleep, so
I will shower you with Zen hugs and kisses and guarantee
their exchange for tangible hugs and kisses, soon. Sweet
dreams, Mindy.
Soon speak,
Edward

From: Mindy
To: Edward
Date: Monday, August 15
Subject: RE: Deal Breakers

~~~Good morning, Edward~~~
... So happy to wake up to your e-mail and read it with
my first cup o' Joe. Very cozy. An excellent way to start
my day. Sounds like it was a nice evening for you and
your dancing feet. Happy that there were a couple of deal
breakers to keep you from getting involved with a less than
healthy woman ... even though it is not of her doing. You
need healthiness and happiness this time around. Time for
you to take care of you, my friend.
   Well, sweets, time to start my day. One more week and
then I head out West. And then back here to you and our
freeway tryst! Very fun to ponder ...
Have a great day and talk soon, Mindy

From: Mindy
To: Edward
Date: Monday, August 15
Subject: Always So Nice ...

... to hear your voice and feel your energy. It is palpable
☺
Sweet dreams, Edward
Mindy

From: FunMrEdward
To: ClarityNow
Date: Tuesday, August 16
Subject: Cowboy Boots?

Hey Sweetie,
I just cruised thru your profile, curious about your changes.
I didn't see anything about cowboy boots. Did that become
problematic? I like the photos you added. Your talking
about honing the profile prompted me to do a little honing
myself. Trying to prequalify the potential clients who are
paying attention. Those who are not paying attention,
well, whatchu gonna do? We know what to do if they don't
have a photo, now don't we.
   So, what, we don't need no stinkin' badges or cowboy
boots? Go on with your good/bad self girl. Hug you up.
Yes ma'am!
Soon speak,
Edward

From: ClarityNow
To: FunMrEdward
Date: Tuesday, August 16
Subject: Re: Cowboy Boots?

Hey you,   :-)
Decided to delete the cowboy boots ... I was attracting an odd crowd. Still love 'em, though. Guess I will leave their appearance in my life to happenstance. I'm glad you like the photos. I need to get more, I guess. Although, to me, I look the same in all of them and how many times you can you post the same damn smile??!! Smiling makes me look infinitely energetic and younger so, luckily, I do smile and laugh a lot in person, as well ... Also funny you should mention my pictures as I was just wondering while driving home tonight if we will appear the same to each other as we do in our heads ... even though we have pictures. It will be interesting on so many levels. Good on you for being the brave soul you are ... WE are. Look at us! Talk soon,
Mindy

From: ClarityNow
To: FunMrEdward
Date: Tuesday, August 16
Subject: You are so funny ...

My dear sweet Edward ... just read your adapted profile and love it. You have such a unique way with words. You write like you talk, which is so happy-provoking. You rock.
Mindy

From: FunMrEdward
To: ClarityNow
Date: Tuesday, August 16
Subject: Re: You are so funny ...

Dear Sweet Mindy,
Thank you girl. Thank you for being the brave blurting soul that helped us both be brave. Yes, look at us. I am so looking forward to the view. Okay, okay, "Be Here Now" ... Huuuummmmm, oops, Ooommmmm. I'm not distracted yet.

Your boots were attracting an odd crowd, eh? Was it the Pony Play crowd? People who are sexually excited by dressing and acting like horses, and their riders? Go figure. I saw that on an HBO sex special series. A great deal of different ways people get stimulated. Whatever blows smoke up your skirt.

So, if you are online now, give me a call if you please. Soon speak, hopefully.
Edward

From: ClarityNow
To: FunMrEdward
Date: Wednesday, August 17
Subject: "Brave, blurting soul" ... Tourette's perhaps?

Good morning, Edward!
Up early to gird my loins and fight the good fight. Or a reasonable facsimile ... not sure, exactly, how one gird's their loins ... come to think of it ... hmmm.

Thank you for the wonderful chat last night. Time flies when I am listening to your voice! I find it to be very grounding.

So much to do before I leave town. I am struggling to "be here now" ... which is my journey this time around, apparently. That and a few other things, I am thinking.

Have a safe day at work. Let me know if you buy your motorcycle ... very exciting! I know you would love to have it now, sooner, rather than later. Especially since the weather will be getting nicer as we get closer to fall.

Keep me posted. Talk soon, sweets!
Mindy

From: Mindy
To: Edward
Date: Wednesday, August 17
Subject: Freak flag flying

Dear Edward,
I was thinking of your 'younger you' photo and wondered if you saw my photos taken circa mid-70's on Facebook? Maybe that will jog your memory on whether or not we slept together in another life.
Hugs and all that other good stuff,
Mindy

From: Edward
To: Mindy
Date: Wednesday, August 17
Subject: Plethora of Activity, and yet ...

Dear Mindy,

Thank you for the multiple messaging. It's always good to hear from you, sweet.

Upcoming itinerary: Get STD and HIV testing done, for myself and a dear friend. I intend to take care of that in the next few days.

And then, my calendar is marked with "Mindy to WA State" and a line starting on Saturday and going off the page and into the next month. And then, "Mindy's back." And then, "Mindy is in Ashland!!!" to visit with a dear friend (anybody I know?). Nice calendar. Wonderful stuff. My head is spinning, just from reading all this stuff. Poor baby. I am a very lucky fellow.

"Mindy!" three weekends away. Oh frabjous joy!

So, sweet lady, I bid you adieu and sweet dreams. Zen hugs and kisses, redeemable for more substantial items. Have a great day, taking care of bidness. Be there now, tomorrow. Soon speak, Dear.

Edward

From:	Mindy
To:	Edward
Date:	Thursday, August 18
Subject:	Always So Nice ...

Good morning, Edward ... so nice to have your missive waiting at this early hour. ☺ Love 'talking' to you over coffee ... does my heart good.

You are one busy dude! Lots of emotional stuff going on around you. Funny to have so much going on and still feel the hole of someone missing to be busy with. I know that feeling. It is easy for me to get caught up with emotional wanderlust and miss what is right before my eyes. Life. Standing in the freaking hallway, waiting for a door (even a doggie door!) to be thrown open to illuminate the next "steps" of my journey.

Just don't run off and get married before our weekend, sweet man. ☺

Here is something that was suggested to me and was a clarifying exercise: make a list of 100 words that describe your "perfect partner." It sounds daunting but it is very illuminating and you don't have to do it all at one sitting. I have three lists on the desktop of my computer: My Perfect Partner, My Perfect Place, and My Perfect Work. I read them every day and tweak them ... add a word, use a better word for a particular characteristic, etc. What it does is add clarity to my intuitive self and lets my subconscious "do the shopping." Fine-tuning the winking-in of a mate. Perfect. Make your list; check it twice. Let Santa bring you what your heart desires.

Time to get ready for work. Your days/nights are very busy. I have dinner tonight with friends. Friday night I will be home packing like a mo'fo', Saturday morning up early to go into DC for acupuncture, leave for airport around 3pm, fly out to PDX, arrive Portland around 8:30 PDT, find my driver to take me to Longview, hug on my parents, and go to bed. Think about you. Think about our weekend. Stay in the NOW of being with my folks/family/friends.

Have an ab-fab day, Edward ... talk soon, sweets.
Mindy

CHAPTER 13

MINDY:

Although I feel brave and excited about setting up the meeting with Edward, the fact that it is 3 weeks in the future gives me lots of time to create an interminable inner list of "what ifs?"

I see this meeting as both a chance to heal and an opportunity to overcome fears around my own perceived sexual shortcomings. I think I used to be good at this. From my many conversations with Edward, I trust he will be a great reminder and a wonderful teacher. I long to give and receive intimacy in all of its forms. It has been years since I have done either.

I am ready to relax my single-minded nature and trust that I am ready for whatever lessons come my way. Life is too short. I want to learn all I can this time around. No regrets. Even for the pain I may cause myself by running willy-nilly into this adventure. Feeling a broken heart is better than not feeling at all.

The thought of getting old and having new sex is so weird. However, Edward is all about it. The cool thing is that we still talk about the other people we are pursuing in our "real" lives. We have the conversation about how we will be after the sex weekend ... that it might be difficult to see each other head off with other folks ... but have decided that we can do this.

To this end, I text Edward the following lines and hit "send" before I have time to chicken out:

Friday, August 19 - Phone Texts

Mindy: It has been a long time since I've had sex with anyone but me ... is it like riding a bicycle? Will you be my training wheels?

Edward: Oh Lady, I do believe it is like riding a bicycle from the "how to" aspect. I will be your relearning wheels if you will be mine. Looking forward to studying together.

Mindy: We are beyond brave.

Edward: Of course we are. But it is so much easier with a dear friend. I want you to bring your toys with you.

Mindy: "Toys?"

Edward: "Yes, adult toys. Don't you have any? Do we need to go shopping? I am all about your satisfaction and how many ways we can find it. I like exploring and I think you will also."

MINDY:

I hope we can be this upfront when we are actually face to face. Of course, since Edward drinks, he can always do that to calm his nerves ... I, on the other hand, will just rely on his mellowness to keep me calm.

The conversations around this meeting are very exciting. We are simultaneously on our computers and on the phone with each other. Edward finds a hotel that seems nice. We talk about the wisdom of getting a suite so we have a lot of room to ... what? ... I don't know ... I don't even like sharing a bathroom with someone I know, let alone a man I have never met.

The nervousness I am beginning to feel has nothing to do with second thoughts on meeting Edward. Rather, it is my old nemesis, that I am not good enough, cute enough, skinny enough, and attractive enough for anyone. Old baggage is rearing its ugly head. I am struggling with old self-worth phantoms. I had these feelings when I was a teenager. I am currently 59. Shoot me now.

EDWARD:
DEJA VU-ish

So now, this lovely young woman, who lives too far away and is not the right woman for the rest of my life, with whom I get along and carry on so freely and comfortably, has invited me to meet her halfway, and also, all the way. We have talked about getting a suite with a bed and a sofa bed so we do not have to sleep together. I have assured her that I am a gentleman and capable of sleeping in the same room with her, and sleeping only. I know I can do it. I know I can. It could turn out that we don't like each other after all, despite our many pleasant phone conversations. We could meet and share our bodies as intimately as we have shared our minds and spirits. Be brave young man, be brave. Trust for the best. How much we will share is still an unknown. But discovering the unknown is part and parcel of us meeting in person anyway.

I am highly flattered and honored that she would even entertain thoughts of sharing with me, much less actually ask me to join her in the mutual undertaking of relearning how to share bodies with another person. Huge compliment ... huge responsibility ... huge concern and self doubt. What if I don't make her happy, satisfied? And after all our talk, what then. This could turn out great. This could turn out as a great fiasco. Crud. (Think positively, Edward.) This is a great opportunity, and Mindy could like it too.

EDWARD:
My Mother, Betty Friedan and Germaine Greer

My father was in the Army, a Protestant chaplain, in fact. He didn't bring the Army home with him from work. And the religion, well, my parents were seriously practicing, but again, it was lived but not proselytized. I certainly received my indoctrination but was ultimately allowed to make my own choices.

My mother and father got along well, didn't fight at all, had some common interests and had some individual interests. It was a time in the world when all parents were allowed and expected to "parent" any and all children who came into their realm of charge at any particular moment. It takes a village to raise a child, if you remember.

Out of my growing up, I always held my mother in the same regard as my father, woman and man. Neither was more dominant than the other. They were of equal importance. And so, I always considered women to be equal to, as good, and as important as me.

I graduated from high school in 1968. I read Betty Friedan's "The Feminine Mystique" that year and then "The Female Eunuch" by Germaine Greer in 1971. There was a great deal going on in the world around us at that time. A part of that was the public and vocal supposition that women had been repressed, held down in societal, sexual and economic terms, and that was not right, as humans dealing with each other. It made perfect sense to me. Folks are folks, womenz and menz, we all want and need pretty much the same things from life. The fact that most womenz and menz did not speak about this between themselves just exacerbated the problems and the non-understandings. And that made both groups the losers. What a shame and waste of time, space and potential for joy shared.

It took me a few years but I did come to understand the distinction and separation of sex and love. It is nice when they concur but it is not mandatory for either existence. And I realized that it should be a long way from "That feels good" to "I love you."

From: Edward
To: Mindy
Date: Friday, August 19
Subject: Hot Date Friday Night

Dear Mindy,
Thanks for being my hot date tonight. Much more fun to visit with you than to go out and about. Say, aside from zydeco, what kind of music do you enjoy? I know I should know this but it escapes me at the moment.

Somehow I never did finalize my hopes and dreams for the future. Neither out loud with you nor inside my head, aside from the interest in a lady love.

Beyond that, I am still limited in that I need to work a few years. I still don't know what I want to be when I grow up. I need to work on a list to help my own awareness and direction. Thank you for enhancing my awareness on this. I am reminded that it's not so important what one is doing. It's more relephant as to whom you are doing it with, which goes back to the top of the list. Talk about making stuff up as we go along. It's important to be able to do that.

What are your hopes and dreams, my dear friend? Do you have a clue just yet?

Of the collective men you have viewed on the site, what percent were attractive enough to catch your eye? On my side of the view, I would say 5%, maybe 10%. Slim pickins. Oh well, that's 5 to 10 % more than doing nothing, eh? And if you play your cards right, you can hook up with a guy with fish. Oh yeah. How come none of the girl pictures are holding fish? Should I feel left out? I'll try to buck up.

Hey sweetie, it's past my bedtime again so I'm headed for horizontal. Soon speak.

Sweet dreams and hugs and kisses.

Edward

From: Mindy
To: Edward
Date: Saturday, August 20
Subject: RE: Hot Date Friday Night

Dear Edward,

Yes, I very much enjoy our dates. I could listen to your voice and hear your thoughts for hours ... which is pretty much how long we chat, come to think of it! Nice.

As to music, I love all kinds ... don't know anything about and really don't listen to country ... just never think about it. My brother was an opera singer and taught me the love of that. Pretty much anything but heavy metal and rap. And baroque ... for some reason, baroque makes me cranky. Used to have a roommate many years ago who constantly played baroque music and both she and the music got on my last nerve.

I am pretty clear on my hopes and dreams, as I perceive them. I try to not limit the universe and all its goodness but, basically, like yourself, I want to have a partner for loving, laughing and sharing. I want to live on the ocean again … I found it to be very healing when I lived next to the ocean in South Florida. The salt water and salt air were so wonderful for me physically and emotionally. Don't like mountains so much, except for visiting. Like high desert country more, again for visiting from time to time. I get depressed and despondent when I am in drizzly, cloudy weather … which is why I only visit WA State in the summer months.

I want the freedom to be able to do what I want. I want to NOT have to suit up and show up at a job every day but I DO want meaningful work and direction in my life. I want the ability to pick and choose how/where I spend my time. I want to be of service to others. I want to laugh and dream and love with someone. I want to be financially independent. My brother always says, "money gives you options" … I always want to have options. Since my divorce I have had this fear of being a bag lady … that is why I have worked so hard these past several years. That fear has lessened but I was raised to be able to take care of myself. Sometimes I think that is my lesson this time around: to know that I am good enough and strong enough to take care of myself AND to have the faith that the universe will provide and "everything is perfectly perfect."

My parents have set a good example of how to not think

of illness and crankiness as a natural part of aging. They are pretty ageless. That is another reason, I suppose, that I think of myself as being much younger than I am. I still have parents that participate in life so I still feel like a kid.

Well sweets ... I need to get my packing done and make last minute preps for heading out later today. My friend is picking me up at 3:30 to drop me at the airport ... which is only 10 minutes away. Very convenient. I will give you a call at 11am today and, hopefully, will have made some serious progress towards my departure.

Hugs and Talk soon,

Mindy

CHAPTER 14

MINDY:

I am scheduled to visit my parents in the Pacific Northwest from August 22 to September 5. Having blurted out my "training wheels" offer my brain is abuzz with my future meeting with Edward. I am still totally comfortable with the idea of meeting a man I have never met in person, in a strange hotel in a town I have never been to. And sharing a bathroom. And bodily functions. More or less. For an inherent worrier and self-second-guesser, the fact that I am not running screaming for the hills (or curled up in a fetal position) tells me that on some deep level this is SO what I am supposed to do. I never feel this sure about anything. I feel settled and in my own skin. Present. Not mind-numbingly dreamy/smarmy. For once I am going to get out of my head and into my body; and my body is telling me this is a GREAT idea.

We speak daily on the phone regarding our impending meeting. Okay. Tryst. It is becoming apparent to me that Edward is a planner and is taking my training wheels request very seriously on all levels. I am beyond flattered. No one has paid this much attention to me in years, if ever … and it is all so romantic. He wants everything to be perfect. As do I, but he is much more organized in his thought process.

We talk about everything and every possibility that may (or may not) occur during our weekend-o-love. Snacks? Check. Candles? Check. Music? Check. Condoms? Check. Since we don't have the results for Edward's STD test we are acting like adults and playing the game correctly regarding safe sex. Back in the day, of course, a dose of penicillin would cure anything. Not so much anymore. We are being safe.

Edward has a huge love and fascination for music of all kinds. It is agreed that he will bring the music. I am the last living person that still owns a boom box so I will bring that. We aren't terribly high-tech … alas, no iPod or even anything remotely resembling one. We will be each other's focus. With a few snacks thrown in.

In all of this idyllic planning the thought occurs to me (somewhere between the "what kind of cheese do you enjoy?" and "what type of chocolate do you prefer: milk or dark?") that Edward may be bringing a bottle of wine. It is the only thing that seems to be missing in this whole scenario and, of course, I don't drink. Nor do I want to be in a hotel room with a man who is drinking around me. I send the following e-mail with a heavy heart knowing that my training wheels session may come to a screeching halt before it has even begun. I e-mail Edward:

From: Mindy
To: Edward
Date: Saturday, August 20
Subject: An important question

Dear Edward,
I was just struck by a thought brought on by your generous picnic planning … will there be alcohol involved? The reason I ask is that, of course, I won't be drinking it but will you? And, if so, I am not sure how I feel about that. I would never tell you when or not to drink … but I do think that our sexual encounter and all that entails could be a particularly slippery slope for me given the mixture of excitement, trepidation

100

and just wanting to ease my nerves in general. I don't mean to assume anything, but I do need to talk about this with you. I know you don't understand my being in recovery, but it is something I staunchly protect. I don't know if I trust myself to be around you, in a hotel room, with alcohol. Is this a deal breaker, my friend? Talk soon, Mindy

MINDY:

A long phone conversation ensued and it was stated that there were no thoughts of bringing alcohol. Whew.

EDWARD:

In a phone conversation this evening, I assure Mindy that alcohol will not be a part of our picnic supplies. That thought hadn't even crossed my mind. She is relieved and feels better. Consequently, I'm relieved because she feels better. Good for both of us.

MINDY:

At this point I fly out to Washington State to visit my family. Due to the 3-hour time difference it is difficult to connect with Edward via phone. We do, however, text a lot! There is much "to-ing and fro-ing," as well as excitement building because when I return from this trip our meeting will take place. It is all very heady and makes my heart happy. I am so excited!

During this time, most of our communication is through phone conversations and texts.

Sunday, August 21 - Phone Texts

Edward: Sweet Mindy, I am so looking forward to kissing you all over!

Mindy: Yum on the kissing all over scenario :-)

Edward: Carly Simon = Anticipation!

Mindy: Haha! We need to appreciate the anticipation ... but it IS making me crazy; in a good way, of course...

Monday, August 22 - Phone Texts

Edward: Mindy girl ... tell me which side of the bed you sleep on. I am good either way; I am ambisleeperous.

Mindy: LOL!!! Ambisleeperous ... you are so clever/funny!!

Edward: You have mentioned jammies. I am intrigued. What are your jammies like?

Mindy: Jammies equate to a t-shirt. I am not a frilly jammie girl. Generally becuz I am the only one who sleeps w/ me. :-(

Edward: A t-shirt jammie sounds excellent.

Tuesday, August 23 - Phone Texts

Edward: Hey girl ... Kiss you all over!

Mindy: Mmmmmm ... nice squirmy thoughts indeed ...

From: Mindy
To: Edward

Date: Tuesday, August 23
Subject: Earthquake

Are you okay?

From: Edward
To: Mindy
Date: Tuesday, August 23
Subject: Re: Earthquake

Hey Sweetie,
We are fine. A lot of talk on the news but I didn't notice anything.

Epicenter was between Charlottesville and Richmond, 5.8 on the scale.

I don't really know how severe that is. Been a long time coming, but an ongoing possible. We are fine. Okay if I call you?

From: Mindy
To: Edward
Date: Tuesday, August 23
Subject: Re: Earthquake

Sweets,
Thanks for calling and putting my mind at ease ... didn't mean to be abrupt ... there is a small daily window of opportunity when I can get my folks in the car and out to do appointments so was in the midst of trying to do that. Quite like herding cats except they tucker out much more

quickly. Talk soon. Good to hear your voice mid-day. :-)
Smooch you, Mindy

From: FunMrEdward
To: ClarityNow
Date: Tuesday, August 23
Subject: Coming Home Early!

Dear Mindy, It is a disappointment to not be able to speak
at leisure like we do, but it is not a problem. I am sorry
things are so rocky for you. I may be wrong but I suspect
something like that. So I feel bad for you dear. So, we will
speak tomorrow and try to make it better.

Hug you up, kiss you all over, sleep in your embrace.
Sweet dreams lady. Now the question is, can I get to sleep.
I will be brave. I am also ready to reserve another night.
Yummmm.

Sweet dreams dear. Soon speak.
Edward

From: ClarityNow
To: FunMrEdward
Date: Tuesday, August 23
Subject: Re: Coming Home Early!

If I told you what it was about you would no doubt laugh.
Happy your kind self understands. You are an exceptional
man Mr. Edward.
Spoon you baby!
Mindy

PS: I am typing this on my phone. These smart phones really ARE smart!

Talk soon. :-)

CHAPTER 15

From: FunMrEdward
To: ClarityNow
Date: Wednesday, August 24
Subject: Sweet Dreams

Hey Sweetheart,

As ever, I enjoyed our conversation this evening. I just added Saturday night to our reservations. Same confirmation number. I still like the same arrival plan. 11 AM, isn't that what we decided? Time for lunch. Bring your bathing suit, just in case we want to swim laps. Okay, more excitement my dear. Thank you for stirring it up. Thank you for stirring us up. Hug you up and smooch you all over. Yes ma'am. Smooch. Sweet dreams.

Edward

From: ClarityNow
To: FunMrEdward
Date: Wednesday, August 24
Subject: Re: Sweet Dreams

My mantra = 3 words: Hooray for us! :-)

EDWARD:
Anti-Social Diseases

Part of the responsible side of our conversations, especially since we have decided to meet for Training Wheels sessions, is the reality of anti-social diseases and the need to be tested for such. I've been with two women in the past thirty year time period, and I know in my heart that I don't have any STD's (sexually transmitted diseases), but any rational new sexual partner would be remiss in not wanting scientific proof of that fact. I want that assurance myself.

Mindy assures me that she's been tested since any sexual contact and that the results are negative. I didn't see the test results paperwork but I'm confident that her statement is the truth. The onus is upon me to go collect the same testing and results, so Mindy and I can meet for Training.

I have noticed a local hospital group has a country outpost, testing lab and emergency care facility, conveniently located on the way home from my work. One afternoon I stop and go in. When asked how they can help me, I tell the receptionist that I want to get tested for STD's. She tells me that I need a referral from my doctor before they "can" do my testing. I assure her that I am of the age of consent and have health insurance plus cash, to insure payment. I don't need permission or a note from anyone but me. They don't agree with my perception of my supposed control of my own destiny. They insist that they must have a note from my doctor. I'm not pleased, but they don't offer to arm wrestle me for it, so I go on my way without further discussion.

The next day I call my doctor's office. Of course, you don't get to speak with the doctor. You have to leave a message, sometimes with a machine, sometimes with a person, and then you wait for a return call. I left my request for a referral to such-and-such labs for my STD testing. I have a new girl friend and I'm being a responsible adult and human. My phone call is to my personal physician, my family doctor, someone who's supposed to be helpful and have my best interests at heart. At least that's my thinking/feeling about who and how this is supposed to be. When the nurse returns my call, she tells me that I need to make an appointment to see the doctor for counseling before he will make the referral for my STD lab testing. And the soonest appointment available is three weeks away. (Heck, I'm supposed to be meeting my new friend in two weeks ... three weeks and beyond won't work.) I assure her that I'm of age, sound and informed mind, and I don't need to be counseled by the doctor in order for him to share a note with the testing lab. I am emphatically told that a testing referral is not forthcoming any other way. I tell the nurse that I'm disappointed with the doctor, apparently he isn't my personal physician and perhaps I need to find a different doctor. I need/want a personal physician, not a corporate bill stimulator and collector.

I'm most upset when I share this saga with Ms. Mindy. Oh, the corporate greed, the lack of true service and caring in the medical field, oh the gnashing of teeth ... mine. Well, she replies, after listening patiently, "Why not go to Public Health?" Huh? Public health? I do recall the concept, but haven't reconnected with that realization. We often know many things. We don't always realize things we know until we're reminded. Thank you Mindy.

I find the address and phone number for Public Health and phone them the next day. Their testing is done on Mondays or Wednesdays, between 8 AM and 12 Noon, come on down. First come, first served. This is a Thursday. Knowing we will be busy on the job the following Monday, I make arrangements with my boss for me to take off the following Wednesday morning.

The nurse practitioner is pleasant, courteous and helpful. She's happy for my good fortune in finding a new lady friend, and glad that we're being health aware and responsible. Results will be back in two weeks. "What? I'm supposed to be meeting this woman in a week and a half." Results will be back in two weeks. In the mean time, act responsibly. The nurse gives me two dozen condoms as a parting gift, like party favors. Thank her very much, for the gift and the encouragement.

Public Health allowed me to be the adult and make my own decisions about getting tested for STD's, and I thank them for that. And it was very inexpensive. Imagine that. My government helping me be healthy. What a strange concept. It should be the norm.

(Two Weeks Later) When I get the results of my testing, it's as I expect. Negative. No STD's, no anti-social diseases.

The world of STD's today is much scarier than when I first became sexually active. I had my first sexual exchange in 1968, and I thank her very much for preventing me from losing my mind due to frustration. Anyway, back then, if you got an anti-social disease, you went to the free clinic, got a shot of penicillin, and didn't play the game for two weeks. It all worked out quite well and easily. But for some time now, succumbing to your hormonal urges can get you killed. For that reason, I really don't envy single people these days. Oh darn … that includes me.

Thursday, August 25 – Phone Texts
Edward: Hey Mindy, Hope you are having fun being lazy on the West Coast!

Mindy: You are my fun; no time for unfun!

Mindy: Lying in bed ... slowly waking up ... wish you were here...

Edward: Wish I was there to wake up with you ...

Mindy: Smooch you. ;-)

Edward: Smooch you back, and front. :-)

From: Edward
To: Mindy
Date: Thursday, August 25
Subject: Being Craftsy

Hey Dear,
We're getting called to action dear. Bite you now, bite you more later, and not a moment too soon. Kisses. Edward

From: Mindy
To: Edward
Date: Thursday, August 25
Subject: You are indeed a craftsy person!

You really don't bite, do you?
Smooches,
Mindy

From: Edward
To: Mindy

Date: Thursday, August 25
Subject: Nibble, Gobble, Chew

Hey Sweets,
I do bite but only very gently. A soft nibble. I promise, you will like it. Better still, I like to kiss and lick and taste. I promise, you will like it. I'm working myself up, making promises to you.
HURRAY FOR US!!!
  Workday is done, time to head for the house. It's my turn to fabricate supper. Speak later.
Kisses,
Edward

From: Mindy
To: Edward
Date: Thursday, August 25
Subject: RE: Nibble, Gobble, Chew

Hooray for us. Hooray for you being my training wheels ... you are one brave sweet soul my Edward. :-)

Thursday, August 25 - Phone Texts
Mindy: I'll try my best to call and say goodnight. I lean into you, sweets

Edward: We lean into each other dear lady, very nicely it would seem.

Mindy: I'm hoping you will be getting something out of this too

Edward: You know I'm being totally selfish. But if I play my cards right, I think I get the girl!

Mindy: I look forward to hearing more, sweets ... you have a lot of energy around this. Kiss you!

Edward: Sweet dreams dear lady. I save my energy for kissing you ... soon!

Friday, August 26 - Phone Texts

Edward: Mindy!! I am so looking forward to rubbing auras with you! It will be like a Vuja De. We have never been here before.

Mindy: Mmmmmm ... rubbing auras ...!

From:	Mindy
To:	Edward
Date:	Friday, August 26
Subject:	Perspective ...

Sweet Mr. Edward: I love that you have such a positive perspective around things ... like the fact of our time difference: that when I am having coffee you are having lunch ... and that I wake up to a lovely message from you every morning. Our combined energy rocks. Still working on the whole toe scenario, but since you are my training wheels I will consider it. ;-)
Sweet dreams,
Mindy

From: Edward
To: Mindy
Date: Saturday, August 27
Subject: Re: Perspective ...

Sweeet Mindy,

Yes, our combined energy rocks. Thank you for considering the sharing of your toes. No, I do not have a foot fetish. It is probably accurate to say I have a female fetish. All parts are adorable, mind, spirit and body. Toes are just another part that can share such pleasure. Often overlooked and/ or forgotten. My thinking is that anyone who says they do not enjoy having their toes sucked is either a liar or they have never tried it.

There was a line in a movie I saw recently which I like: "There is nothing dirty that can be done if the parts are clean." It was a line by a female character, speaking of bathing before sex. Makes perfect sense to me. So we will start with clean toes and I'm suspecting you will enjoy it. And all of the other clean parts as well. I do know where to start, with your mouth. And we will make it up from there. Here, there, everywhere! Hurray for us!

Okay, so let us keep up the business of not working ourselves into a lather, otay?

Hugs and kisses, girl.

Yummm!

Edward

From: Mindy
To: Edward
Date: Saturday, August 27
Subject: Re: Perspective ...

Dear Edward ... just saw this e-mail ... I find it and you quite squirmifying. I appreciate your candor which is one of the things I love about you. That and your myriad smooching/nibbling innuendos ... yummmm...

Saturday, August 27 - Phone Texts

Mindy: I truly hope that I am as tasty as you imagine me to be...

Edward: I am so looking forward to finding out just how tasty you are!

Mindy: I lean into you, sweet Edward.

Edward: We are leaning into each other, sharing, and finding our comfort there.

CHAPTER 16

Monday, August 29 - Phone Texts

Mindy: SO excited about our weekend! Please don't over-think it ... no pressure on us ... I am saying these things to YOU to remind ME, of course!

Edward: Sweet woman, I am equally excited to meet yourself in the 3-D world!

Mindy: Right now I'm focusing on and setting the intention for our weekend o' sharing. :-)

Edward: To borrow a line from Elvis Costello, "Our aim is true!"

Mindy: You can't imagine how happy I am to be doing this with you ...

Mindy: AND I can't imagine doing it with anyone else ... truly.

Edward: Though most of my recent dating experiences have had funky results, I have no fears for our meeting.

Tuesday, August 30 - Phone Texts

Mindy: I so enjoyed our chat tonight ... will be such fun when we are snuggled and doing it in person. You warm me all over! Have a wunderbar and safe Tuesday sweetness!

Mindy: Morning my truck stop dude! Up and at 'em early as I have much to do today prior to heading to Portland in prep for flying out early tomorrow. Will arrive IAD around 4pm tomorrow. Good to get home and prep for our trucker tryst ...

Edward: I look forward to a truck stop dessert ... I want to eat your peaches, I want to shake your tree!

Mindy: Yummers ...

Edward: May your flight be smooth and the wind at your back. :-)

Mindy: Focusing on us in this moment is much more fun.

From: Mindy
To: Edward
Date: Wednesday, August 31
Subject: Edward!!!!!

I'm home and happy to be so!! You don't have to call on my freakin' cell phone anymore ... yayyyy! I am busily doing laundry, unpacking and scrounging for something to eat. I am a bit pooped but excited for our visit ... now that I am back on this side of the globe it is even more real ... Lordy. Mindy

Thursday, September 1 - Phone Texts
Mindy: Going to look for some cute undies ... wish me

118

luck! Smooch you!

Edward: Oh no, anything but cute undies! Don't throw me into the Mindy patch!

Mindy: Yeppers ... lucky me ... lucky you ... a couple of squirmy lucky ducks. :-)

Edward: I look forward to luckin and duckin with you girl!

Mindy: Getting cute is not for the faint of heart ... just sayin'. B-)

Edward: I know you to be brave of heart and pure of soul.

Mindy: It's a thin line between bravery and insanity ... I trust you are doing this with the best of intentions for both of us ... as am I ... yay us!

From: Mindy
To: Edward
Date: Thursday, September 1
Subject: Some thoughts

My dear sweet Mr. Edward,
I want you to know how much I appreciate our open and honest conversations on so many topics. Do you know that I have had more in-depth conversations around sex,

sexual gratification and body parts with you, a man I have yet to meet, than I have in my ENTIRE life, even with my husband of many years?! Not sure what that says ... maybe that I am just open to talk about and experience things more or that I recognize in you a completely honest and trustworthy man with whom to share. I am pretty sure it is a bit of both. And I appreciate that it is an important part of your helping me remember/re-learn how to do something that I haven't done in a long, long time. Funny that it has taken this long to present itself but I am thinking that I was waiting for a kind heart such as yourself to help me get back on the bicycle.

Everything happens for a reason and I am so happy that you have happened to me, now ... in this moment.

Hugs and kisses, my friend; soon in person!

Mindy

Friday, September 2 - Phone Texts

Mindy: Dancing, frolicking and quite pleased with ourselves :-) smooch on you, sweet Edward!

Edward: Singing like no one is listening, dancing like no one is watching, loving like we have never been hurt before!

Mindy: Ps ... I'll bring lube (for some reason I feel odd texting this to you ... hopefully, no one is reading this over your shoulder ... nice ...)

Edward: Good call. We do not want to run short of the lube of life, the lube for love!

EDWARD:

Being Prepared

In a previous career path, I was a carpenter for many years. I did all types of carpentry, but ultimately ended up specializing in metal studs and drywall. On one of my jobs, I was given a new helper. He was new to the company and seemed fairly new to the work. We were running a metal frame for a ceiling in a parking garage area on the ground floor. It was February and quite cold. We were across the street from a river with a brisk wind whipping through our work space. He had no coat and other than a nail bag, hammer and tape, he didn't seem to have any tools ... not the help I'm looking for. I asked if he had a screw gun. "I used to have a screw gun" he replied. I asked what happened to it. "I sold it at a yard sale" was the response. "No, no, no, you don't sell tools at a yard sale, you buy tools at a yard sale" I told him. "What kind of work did you do before you came out here?" I asked. "I used to fuel jets on an aircraft carrier." I said, "Well, consider coming to work here as if you were going out on that aircraft carrier. If there's anything that you'll need when you get here, be sure to bring it with you or you'll be out of luck." Thankfully, he didn't return to work the next day and made my job much easier. I hope he caught on, for his sake.

I would rather have too much gear than not enough.

MINDY:

Expectations:

I see this meeting with Edward as a both a soothing balm and energizing boon for my spiritually weary ego and body. I have no idea what to expect; I try to not dwell on the outcome. I just know, in my heart of hearts, that this will be an experience not to be missed, for whatever reason.

This meeting is an opportunity to share with a man I feel deeply connected to, even though we have never formally met. Many long conversations with him have led me to this point.

Over the years of singleness, I have created worries and doubts as to my own desirability and ability. If nothing else, I will use this opportunity to hopefully put those fears to rest.

I am not afraid to be alone for the rest of my life, but I would like to know that, given the opportunity, I can respond appropriately should the need arise.

I also want to be a healing element for Edward. We both come to this meeting with different wounds and hopes and expectations. We have talked much about this. Our intentions are clear, open and honest. It is all good.

Our belief is that this will be a one-time event, which also serves to remove the pressure of performance and angst. It is easier to throw oneself into the moment if every moment is finite. No harm, no foul.

Our energy is consolidated and focused. We are both giddy at the prospect.

EDWARD:

For a couple of weeks, Mindy and I plan our meeting, this weekend at the half way point. No, not in a pup tent two miles out of town, thankfully. We both admit to enjoying the creature comforts available in the modern world. And that is all the better to allow us to pay attention to each other … the point of our meeting.

I make a list to be sure to be prepared. I wouldn't want us

to fall over from malnutrition, just in case we cannot make it out of the room. Multiple dark chocolates, two kinds of cheese, olives … green and black, a variety pack of crackers and a couple flavors of juice from my favorite healthy grocery store. Cooler is packed and iced.

Music … two dozen CD's of mostly instrumental, non-interruptive flavors. A touch of rock and something to which we can dance the Carolina Shag, just in case we're inclined. Remember the Carolina Shag? Isn't that where this whole adventure began? Mindy reached out to me, and I effectively (or should I say, ineffectively?) suggested that she sign up for shag dance lessons so she could meet a nice guy. Little did I realize, the nice guy she's going to meet is me.

Clothes, probably enough for a week. Computer with Internet aircard so we can stay in touch with the outside world without having to go there. Beach towels, camera, flashlight, kneepads (remember how little fun it is to have carpet burn, though it was always great fun getting it), I think I have the possibilities pretty well covered. Darn, I forgot my optical visor, for that up close and personal review.

Over the weeks of talk, mental, spiritual, and physical preparation for our meeting, my emotions have run the gamut: simple, innocent joy at meeting this sweet soul with whom I have connected, sexual desire for this attractive woman, personal and male fear about not measuring up to her desires and expectations. EXPECTATIONS. That is an interesting word. There have been times when I had no right to have expectations of the actions of others. There have been times when I had a right to have expectations of the actions of others. Here and now? I'm trying to maintain my only expectation at the fact that we will like each other and enjoy ourselves. If it's worse than that, I'll be surprised and disappointed. If it's better than that, I'll be brave and lucky and grateful.

CHAPTER 17

First Meeting
9/3/11 – 9/5/11
Overnight Suites
Ashland, VA

MINDY:

The drive to Ashland is easy: 7100S to 123S to 95S and take exit 92. It should be a quick journey at this time of year. (This is also the way to the beach for the metro DC throngs that head out every weekend during the summer months.) Before I know it, I am taking the exit off 95S and into the small college town of Ashland. Even with a college there is not much going on here. Except for (in my mind) the *flashing* neon sign that screams: **Overnight Suites ... sex haven for the aged!!** ... in my mind.

Prior to leaving my house, I have re-confirmed with two close friends where I am going and what I will be doing; although, I am not sure myself of what that might be. I am purposely not going down that mental path. They have the hotel name and contact info as well as Edward's full name and contact info. I have promised them both that I will keep in regular contact with them via text and phone. After the fact we all agree that Edward could have been answering their texts while I was tied up somewhere so it would have been wise to agree on a "safe" word. Again, though, I have never had any inkling or gut feeling that there is anything but sincerity on Edward's part or in his heart. I do not feel like I am being groomed to be a victim. Believe me, if anyone can make up drama it is me ... and I have no thought of such.

EDWARD:

Our original plan is to meet at the hotel at 11am and go get lunch. The evening before we talk and set our time back to 1pm (still two hours before the 3 pm check-in time) so as to not be rushed/stressed about having to get such an early start on our day.

The journey is about 100 miles and two hours of travel time. I leave Smithfield about 10:45 to give myself a couple minutes of leeway, but not be too early. About twenty-five miles up the road is the town of Surrey. It's quaint and historical and the location of the Surrey House, a restaurant of long standing and reputation. That's where I first tasted peanut pie, many years prior. On the spur of the moment, I stop at the Surrey House and purchase two pieces of peanut pie as a surprise treat for Mindy and me.

MINDY:
Hotel Arrival

I am in my car waiting for my knees to stop shaking so I can safely stand up. I cannot believe I am here. I am beyond nervous but I also sense an inner calm. I feel brave and excited and exciting. I am not allowing my mind to traverse the "what if" trail. Edward has not yet arrived. I have the reservation information so I can check us in while I wait for him to appear.

The first thing I notice upon entering the lobby is the throng of folks milling around. What?! They all wear matching T-shirts. They all appear to be participants in a weekend **Bible revival.** Holy crap! Is this some sort of joke?!

I gather my wits. Smiling and nodding all around, I walk to the desk and ask for the reservation under Edward's name. I can sense a scarlet "A" forming on my chest. I keep my eyes down. This is ridiculous. And the Bible group is hogging all the lobby seating. And, of course, our room isn't ready. The Bible folks have taken up all the rooms and ours can't be readied until someone checks out.

I can hardly wait for Edward to arrive so we can have a good laugh over this state of affairs. I listen for the distant bugle of the cavalry.

EDWARD:

The route, for me, is half country roads and half interstate. It flows along nicely and I arrive in Ashland without particular event. It's a gorgeous, clear and temperate day. As is often the case with electronic maps, they get you close but not always exactly where you're supposed to be. This is my experience within the final 100 yards of my journey. The directions have me turning right and there's a tree hiding the hotel sign (to the left) which confuses me for a couple moments. I get myself sorted out and pull into the parking lot looking for Mindy's gray SUV. I don't see it (it's the one that's slate gray, effectively black) but park at the far end of the full lot, and head for the lobby.

As I get close to the entrance, Mindy appears from inside. She looks like her pictures. She looks like herself. She is not short. She has a lovely hour glass figure and a radiant smile. And she is there to meet me. I am one lucky duck! We approach, say hello and share a big hug. Grinning from one ear to the other, I am holding her hand. I expected to like the look of her. I did not expect her to be so tall, so lovely, so curvular in all the right places. GRIN!

MINDY:
Edward

He is slimmer than his picture but tall, as I expected. He has wonderful blue eyes and occasional dimples. His silver hair is short and his beard is well trimmed. He has amazing wrists and hands, one of the first things I notice about any man. Not sure where that comes from but I am a sucker for nice wrists and hands. As soon as he speaks I recognize that voice I have grown to trust. He looks and acts far younger than his 60 years. He has a light spirit.

He seems pleased to see me in real life. We hug. We are at a bit of a loss. Our initial meeting is taking place under the eyes of the Bible folks (in a hotel lobby, no less). This lends a disconcerting air of biblicalness (and/or damnation!) to the event. I am pretty sure that is my baggage, though. Edward seems to be unaware of anything but me.

Now we are both waiting in the lobby for our room. It must be apparent to others, especially the hotel staff that we have never met before, AND we are meeting for some surreptitious goings-on.

Edward and I sit scrunched on a wooden hearth beside the faux fireplace in the lobby. All of the real chairs are occupied. Our legs are touching. Everything is touching. Edward is poking my waist. He seems to be enthralled with the fact that I have a waist and actually resemble my photos. We are acting like a couple of kids. Excited to get to our room so we can collapse in laughter over the fact that we booked the only hotel in town with a religious revival in residence.

EDWARD:

As we get inside, I see that the lobby is full of people, milling about in various clumps. They all seem to be sharing similar conversations and T-shirts. I realize that we are in the midst of a large affiliated group, some flavor of religious gathering. Ohhh, can they read my/our mind? Can they read my/our face? Don't pay attention to them, Edward. Go forward toward securing our room.

Mindy has already spoken with the desk clerk about access to our room. First, there is the matter that check-in is not officially open until 3:00 pm, although they would gladly accommodate us if they could. Then, there is the reality that with all these people in the hotel, the staff is busy dealing with the business of making up rooms that have priority over our early access. The hotel will do their best to get our room ready early. In the mean time, relax and wait patiently.

The only unoccupied seating in the lobby is a tiny ledge in front of a fake fireplace. Mindy and I sit together, close because it is a small hearth ... close because I want to be close with her after all this time of sharing at a distance. I can't keep my hands off of her. Between holding her hand, grinning, poking her gently (I hope) in the side (to verify how trim she is ... to verify that she is really there), I probably make a small spectacle of myself. Frankly, I am mostly oblivious of the world and the lobby around me.

The desk clerk tells us when our room is ready, and we trundle ourselves and our gear up to the room. Mindy can pretty much bring all her luggage by hand in one easy trip. I need a gurney and a careful balancing act to get my travelling show up to the room.

MINDY:

Our room is finally ready! I am thinking that the front desk staff can sense our impatience (and totally want to get our excited selves out of their line of vision) so they hastily clean the first available suite. Hooray!

I get my bag. It appears Edward has brought everything but the kitchen sink. I find it endearing that he has come so well prepared with snacks, music, plates, and silverware. I am beyond touched.

EDWARD:

Once inside, we go about setting up our little corner of the world. Mindy has brought the boom box and electric candles. Music setup is established. Food's put away inside or on top of the fridge, as needed. Hanging clothes out of the way. Suitcases are situated and opened for access. The gurney is taken back to the lobby. All of this we accomplish while interspersing conversation, touches, smiles, slight nervousness and … kisses for days. Mindy's profile had requested someone who liked to kiss for days and that caught my attention, being one of those souls. We successfully keep our glasses steamed up for quite a while.

MINDY:

After a brief moment of staring at each other, we kiss. And it is perfect. We are both thrilled (because, of course, we discuss this endlessly over snacks later) that our mouths are so compatible. Edward has a whole theory about this which involves various citrus fruits. Happily, we bask in the sheer joy of "kissing for days" one moment at a time.

EDWARD:

Good Kissers

Everybody thinks themselves to be a good kisser. It's probably mostly true, but it's very important to be kissing someone with a similar size mouth, or a compromising approach. Several months ago I was reminded of this when I met a couple different ladies at the shag dances. There was a mutual interest and we visited (one at a time) and explored the possibilities of us getting together. Neither worked out for us to be a couple but I was reminded of the dilemmas of kissing. Now this Mindy girl, she and I fit just right. Oh, the Languid Lingering of Lips!!! We can kiss for days! Oh darn, good news.

EDWARD:

We talk about going out for lunch, but decide to just snack on the supplies at hand. We eat enough to be not hungry, but not enough to slow us down. Then I remember the peanut pie and present it, pleased with myself for being thoughtful and bringing such a treat. "What's that?" Mindy asks. "Peanut pie! It's very good," I say. "I'm allergic to peanuts. Are you trying to kill me?" she asks. Whoosh … there goes the wind from those sails. Here, I just met the girl and I'm trying to kill her. Well, not knowingly. We don't eat the peanut pie. I tuck it away for later, for me, after our weekend.

Room is settled and stomach is fed. What next? I ask Mindy if she wants to get undressed and meet each other in the bed. She says yes. WOW! We are actually doing this, and we did, most pleasingly.

Past experience has shown that sometimes, mysteriously, a wet spot appears when folks are sharing sex, especially joyous and repeated sex. Throughout history I am sure there has been much controversy over who gets to/has to sleep in the wet spot. I've always been truly grateful for the ladies who have shared with me, and being totally selfish, wanting to be invited back for more, I've always been glad to sleep in the wet spot. Some things aren't much fun unless you get some on you, and this is one of those cases. The beach towels are deployed.

I've heard that the largest sexual organ is the brain and the largest organ of the body is our skin. I'm now blessed by this lovely soul/woman/person sharing her wondrous self with me. Our skin in contact, here, there, trying for everywhere, all at the same time. Caressing, kissing, hugging, tasting, talking, laughing, and loving (though we have not yet shared that word). Our activity is from languid to feverish and back, visiting all places and speeds between. Kissing and tasting this lovely woman from head to toe and back, oh yes, thank you Great Spirit, thank you Mindy!

Throughout our wonderful weekend of sex and talk, we are mindful of the biblical neighbors and make a conscious effort to keep the noise down. I guess we manage that well enough because we don't receive any complaints.

MINDY:
Up One Side And Down The Other

One thing is apparent; this is a man who appreciates a woman's body. Not only that, he takes his job as my training wheels very seriously. My self-consciousness quickly falls away. It has been so long. And I love that Edward seems as honestly and emotionally thrilled about our mutual good fortune as I am. He is considerate, kind and sincere. I actually begin to feel beautiful, desirable and special. It has been so long. And I am so comfortable! With myself, with him, with the whole sharing of body, mind and spirit. I emotionally jump in with both feet; I want to take advantage of this amazing opportunity to explore, learn and revisit my sexuality. I want Edward to be as happy about our brave adventure as I am. We are so pleased with ourselves!

We have had so many specific conversations over the phone for the past couple of weeks; it seems very easy to also have those conversations in person. As requested, I brought my favorite toy. Edward has brought a small … is that a flashlight?!

[Despite the fact that every hour or so my phone announces an incoming text from one of my "sentinel" friends, who have been charged with making sure I am not abducted by an online lunatic. I assure them through texts that I am fine and will keep them posted. I give them specific times that I will text them so they don't worry.]

Between our forays through the sheets, we dine on cheese, crackers and exotic olives. We talk for hours as we snack, nibble and study each other's bodies. We share the common language of a similar age and time. We compare stories and memories and know all of the lyrics to the same songs. Edward is delighted that our frames of reference mesh so well. We chortle, laugh and end each other's sentences. We have been here before in another lifetime. I think we left the room once to have an actual meal in a local café.

EDWARD:

Although the initial invitation sounds like a simple sexual request, that is not the reality of us. We started by falling in "Like." We progressed to "Sharing and Caring in Minds and Spirits," and ultimately incorporated the final aspect of "Sharing our Bodies." A more natural and complete progression, I have not experienced before in any relationship, much less in such a short time.

Sunday, mid-afternoon, we decide that we can collect ourselves and make it out of our room. Go make sure the world is still out there, go get some lunch. I explore online and find a few restaurants in Ashland. We choose one, check the online map, and head out. The restaurant is maybe two miles away and should be fairly straight forward to get to.

We go just up the road, turn left and I'm looking for a particular street where I need to turn right. I'm finally able to read the street sign as I pass it and realize that's the street where I want to turn. I stop the car (there having been no one behind me before), start to put it in reverse to back up, and look up in my rear view mirror just in time to see cars now approaching rapidly. I immediately change my mind about our direction, go forward, and we travel around a couple extra blocks to get to the restaurant. I really know how to impress a woman.

Mindy is, not only a passenger, but an aware passenger in my car. She just saw and understood what's going on and is immediately wondering if she will ever again feel safe riding with me in a car. Me, the fellow she wanted to meet, sight unseen. Is this the red flag she's been looking for? We're glad to have come out of that one, unscathed, except perhaps my reputation.

EDWARD:

Our original plan is to spend one night together. Two nights is the extended plan, fortunately and thankfully. Two nights gives us time to get acquainted and explore, and then make sure we're correct about our "first" impressions. It's probably a good thing that we don't have a third night to share because we would likely turn ourselves into tiger butter.

One of the best parts of our relationship is the fact that we enjoy our conversations as much as we enjoy sharing sex, if not more. It's all the verbal sharing that brought us together in the first place. It has always been important to me to be able to have good talk between rounds of great sex. I've been ridiculed for that by "the guys" I've mentioned it to over the years. Their attitude was "You're getting laid so what do you care if she can carry on an intelligent conversation." Regardless of them, I've always cared. It's as important, if not more, to stimulate the mind as well as the body. And this fabulous reality of Mindy and me is most excellent ... very satisfying!

After our wondrous weekend of meeting and greeting, it is with heavy hearts and leaden feet that we pack our belongings, say our goodbyes and travel back to our respective "real worlds."

MINDY:

The word that comes to mind, when I think of this weekend with Edward, is "sated." Mind, body and spirit. It is kismet, it is karma, and it is one heck of a good idea that just got better. The lull of so much physical and emotional attention after such a long drought is beyond life changing. For me, it is life-affirming on every level. And a complete shot in the arm for my self-esteem and sense of who I am in this moment.

The thought of saying goodbye after all we have shared is difficult and surrealistic. We have come to realize that the lube of life is the emotional, physical and spiritual juice that keeps us young, excited and open to possibilities. We have succeeded in creating a safe zone in a random suite in a never before visited town. Odd and yet not odd. And the fact that I didn't end up stabbed in a ditch is just icing on the cake!

I was ready to go home. I don't think I had another ounce of lust in me. I needed time alone to process, appreciate and ponder what had transpired over the past few days. I felt enveloped in an emotional hangover and I needed my own space to get back into my body. There is no sadness. Yet.

CHAPTER 18

Monday, September 5 - Phone Texts

Mindy: EDWARD!!! Winding down and wondering where you are. I gots an itch that only you can scratch. ;-) My bad ... I know I should be better than this. I promise I will be ... getting back to work will help alleviate the squirmaliciosness of you, my sweets. Smooch you!

Edward: That's easy for you to say, toying with my emotions from way over there.

Mindy: Remember how I said I want to lean into you? I've changed my mind ... I want to GRIND into you. ;-)

Edward: Hey girl, come over here and recline beneath my face. :-)

Mindy: I know you dislike texting AND you need to rest up for the work week so I will smooch you from here and say good night. The bed will seem lonely ... I will miss snuggling into sleep with you.

Mindy: Ps ... I will get better with this ... promise ... but for right now I really want to bask in us ... at least for a bit longer ... smooch you. :-P

Edward: On one hand, we just met. On the other hand, it does feel strange sleeping, not with you. Good night dear.

EDWARD:
Reality Check

A major premise of Mindy and I meeting is that we are just going to visit one time. Logically knowing that we are not the long-term folks for each other, but emotionally not wanting to chance missing out on sharing intimacy/intimately before we each leave this world, we choose to meet for the "Training Wheels Program," but only once. Romance, quirky mayhem, emotion, logic, being goofballs ... yea verily, sounds like Mindy and me.

Mindy and I are both having a difficult time trying to align our logical minds and the "One Visit Theory" with our emotions and the wonderful exchange of selves and souls during our weekend of initial meeting.

After our most excellent weekend, back in our individual realities, I realize that I want more time and space with this special woman and it seems to be a mutual feeling. So when we got home, we each freak out!!! "Please ma'am, may I have some more?" "I expected to like her. I did not expect to like her so much!" These words would be repeated many times over.

From: Edward
To: Mindy
Date: Monday, September 5
Subject: Lost Weekend

Sweet Mindy
Thank you dear, for finding our lost weekend. All of the sweet words, thoughts and observations shared are true forever. It just occurred to me, I need to go into recovery

from you/us. Damn! And just what you need ... another meeting to go to. I started writing this just before our texts. Now I am verklempt. I pulled out a bottle of whiskey to have a shot, to medicate myself. But I realized you are in the same places as I am, and you are dealing without a bottle, so I put it back unopened. If you are that brave, I will try to be as well.

I remind myself to dwell on the joy. Thank you forever for sharing yourself and our joy with me.

Sweet dreams dear. Soon speak.

Edward

From: Mindy
To: Edward
Date: Monday, September 5
Subject: Re: Lost Weekend

Dear Sweet Edward,

Your awareness and words leave me speechless. You truly are a remarkable man and I am so lucky to have spent such wonderful time with you in such an intimate way. I know we are both better for it, although I'm not sure yet how that 'betterness' will manifest itself in our lives. But ... for sure ... it is a big deal and I am forever indebted to your courage, kindness and amazing honesty with me. I am forever changed, sweetness. Yes, we need to dwell in the joy and specialness of our coming together in every sense of the word.

Sleeping without you tonight will be odd and lonely. But knowing that you are going through the same feelings makes it somehow more palatable.

Sweet dreams.

Talk soon,

Mindy

Xoxoxoxo

Tuesday, September 6 – Phone Texts

Mindy: Smooch your lips, sweet Edward ... be safe at work
... I feel you with, on, in me! So amazingly happy and
grateful for spending our found lost weekend together. I
am so smiling right now ... hug your wonderful body and
smooch you up for good measure.   :-*

Edward: Hey sweetness. You sure know how to get a guy
off to a good start in the morning. Smooch you back, and
front. :-)

Mindy: OMG ... so weird to be back to work. I feel like
everyone can tell I spent the weekend in bed w/you ...
having a hard time looking the guys in the eye. ;-)

Edward: Mindy, maintain faith in yourself, look everyone
straight in the eye, smile and act innocent. Clear questions
from your mind and the questions won't appear in
the minds of others. In the mean time, we know how
wondrous our weekend was! Thank you dear!

Mindy: Even your texts make me tingle ... Lordy, man!!
Heading into a meeting ... I will try to remember to look
them in the eye ...

Mindy: What a day ... where are you??? I need to smooch on you and get lost in some serious humming. ;-)

Edward: Do you mean some serious "Oooommmmmming" my sweet lady, my tender lover?

Mindy: Oooohhh ... "lover" ... that gives me the squirms ... mmmmmm.

Mindy: Sweets, thank you for reminding me that I am love-able. Good sleep, my friend.

Edward: You are most lovely and do not doubt the fact that you are loveable. And such a pleasure to share with my dear!

Mindy: Thank you for saying so, sweet Edward. Just got your text message. I was on the phone. Too sleepy to make any sense so will head to bed now. Smooch your face, my hotel love dude. :-*

Edward: Smooch you back, and front, from top to bottom, my hotel love dudette!!

Mindy: Hahaha ... funny man. :-D I am beyond tired for some reason ... the excitement (for lack of a better word) of going back to work combined with the emotional letdown following our heady love fest, I am thinking. In the meantime I will head to bed with thoughts of being "done" by you on the altar-o-love. UmmmmmmS

Wednesday, September 7 – Phone Texts

Mindy: I miss you. I miss us.

Edward: I am missing our excellent selves together as well, my dear.

Mindy: I kiss your lips. I feel your tongue. Sweet dreams, Edward.

Edward: Mindy, you are my sweet dreams, dear lady. Nights…

EDWARD:

In conversation on the phone tonight, we decide that there is no reason set in stone that we can't get together again. We just want to double check our first impressions. It is still possible that we don't like each other. By the way, who ever thought it was a good idea to just visit once? Couldn't be me, couldn't be she. Our senses must have been clouded by outside forces. Alien abduction?

Friday, September 9 – Phone Texts

Mindy: Checking in ... my brain is fried ... but happy to think about seeing you soon. Yaayyyy us! B-)

Mindy: Are you still taking Monday off?

Edward: I am going to take off Friday at lunch time and Monday as well.

Mindy: Holy crap ... are you serious?

Edward: Just making sure we have time to find out if we dislike each other or not.

Mindy: We blurt well together, my friend ... smooch on you, sweet Edward.

Edward: Mindy, we are the Bold and the Blurtiful! Nibbling your all over!

CHAPTER 19

MINDY:
Reality Check

Edward and I have agreed all along that we are going to continue to look for dates in our own necks of the wood. Somehow, I am (more or less) able to emotionally accommodate this huge juxtaposition (the word DENIAL comes to mind) but, every now and then, reality rears its ugly head and I remember that Edward is going on dates with women that aren't ME and that he may well find the love of his life in someone else.

He is very upfront and honest about these forays, as am I with him. After awhile it begins to border on the unhealthy as we download our dating experiences with each other. For me, it is morbid curiosity tinged with the opportunity to weigh myself against the other women he is meeting. For a woman with self-esteem issues, this is not a good way to go.

I believe that for Edward, and his helpful nature, it is a way of encouraging me to look for a man that is closer to my town. We both continue to "tweak" our online profiles in hopes of finding "the one" but secretly hoping (at least I am) that "the one" is us and we will find a way to work things out.

> From: Mindy
> To: Edward
> Date: Friday, September 9
> Subject: Dates

Dear sweet Edward,
I just need to say this aloud to you: It is FREAKING me

out that you have THREE dates this weekend. Okay. I feel better now. Well. Not really. But I did want to say that in case you thought I didn't care. I do. Having said that, good luck with your dates ... let me know if anything changes regarding our next weekend. I get that could happen. I am trying to not think about it.

Mindy

xoxoxo

Saturday, September 10 – Phone Texts

Mindy: Good morning, sweets ... my a/c stopped working. :-(Getting ready for hours of smiling and yammering at folks. Need to take off my cranky pants and remember that this is what I do. Right now. In this moment. Be here now, Edward. Smooch you.

Edward: Yes dear, Be There Now. Paying attention and doing what needs to be done to go forward and prosper. Kiss you soon!

Mindy: I get to leave event @ 1:30 today so I can meet a/c guy ... yaayyyy ... no more cranky sweaty pants! Well, still sweaty ... but that has more to do with you. ;-)

Edward: I volunteer to help you get sweaty. Otay?

Mindy: Squirmalicious.

Edward: Hey girl, I am off to my lunch date at the beach. Will talk with you later. Rest easy. I am not dipping out.

Mindy: Smooch you ... have fun ... I think. ;-)

Mindy: OMG ... I just picked up my phone and here you are on the other end ... great minds think alike ... so happy to hear you aren't running off with someone else!

EDWARD:

This last comment has to do with the turn of events with today's meeting with Date Lady #6, the second of three dates this weekend. We have spoken on the phone a couple times. Okay, not magic, but she seems like a nice woman. She resides in West Virginia (way too far away), but is passing through Virginia Beach for a couple days and wanted for us to meet, regardless of our disconnects.

We meet at a restaurant that I like and it is close to where she and her travel companion/girl friend are staying. As we are finishing our lunch, she gets a call on her cell phone which she needs to take. Turns out, it is her recently exed boyfriend calling to tell her he is on his way (from Washington DC) to Virginia Beach to make his amends with her. She begs out of our plans to go enjoy music at the blues weekend, happening at the beach. I am not sure what her mood is. I am slightly relieved and pleased to have the afternoon back. I take care of other errands and go have supper with my son. I never see or hear from this woman again. I hope it works out well for her, whatever direction it takes.

Saturday, September 10 – Phone Texts Continued

Edward: No, sweetheart, I am not running off with anyone else. What a relief for me. Kiss you up!

Mindy: Smooch you twice!

Mindy: OMG ... a/c guy was just here ... can't fix it today. Totally putting my cranky sweaty pants back on. :-(

Edward: Sorry you have to be cranky. I would totally like to help you get happy sweaty! Bite you gently. :-)

Mindy: Will try to fix it tomorrow. I may need a whole new system! WTF? Have fun with Britt ... I am here to call when you get back home. Smooch you baby!

Edward: Will give a call when I get home dear. :-*

Sunday, September 11 – Phone Texts
Edward: I am on the road to Richmond. Chat you up later.

Mindy: Just arrived DC. Thinking of you. Smooch you all over. Talk later. Have fun at the train show. :-)

EDWARD:

Today, Sunday, I am visiting with Date Lady #7. She reached out to me through the The Dating Site a couple weeks ago. We have enjoyed our exchanges via e-mail and telephone. Today I am going to meet her in person. She is the activities director at an assisted living facility and they are having a model train display today.

Sunday, September 11 – Phone Texts Continued

Mindy: Just got home from DC ... call when you can.
Xoxoxo

Edward: Will call when I get home sweets! I am on the road.

Edward: I want to hear what's up with our next visit!

Mindy: Call you in a few.

Edward: Come on down, girl!

Mindy: Did I freak you out when I said the love word? I
didn't mean to over step a boundary.

EDWARD:
The "L" Word

In phone conversation this evening, at some point, Mindy
said, "I love you." Without thought, hesitation or guile, I
responded, "I love you." It was perfect and it was true. How
did this happen, while we weren't looking? We have gone and
fallen in love ... oh darn, good news?

MINDY:
The "L" Word

The word "love" just kind of happened in the middle of my
conversation with Edward. It seemed a natural thing to say.
We have shared so much and are such kindred spirits that I
do feel love for him on many levels. So, as I am wont to do,
I blurted it out. I certainly didn't do it to see if he would say

it back to me. At least I don't think so. But I am comfortable with saying it and feel good about doing so. For I truly do love Edward and all that he has shared with me. How could I not?

CHAPTER 20

Monday, September 12 - Phone Texts

Mindy: OMG ... I just accidentally sent your morning smooch message to my boss!!! :-[

Edward: Smooth move girl. Just how intimate are you texting this morning?

Mindy: Hahaha ... maybe I'll get a raise. :-D

Edward: Maybe you'll get a rise.

Mindy: Thankfully I didn't mention any body parts. :-[

Mindy: Smooch you all over sweets ... have an ab-fab day. Be safe. Please come home with all your parts and pieces and intact ... yaayyy us!

Mindy: Hug you up one side and down the other ... kisses 4 you. Just got to the office; I am girding my emotional loins!!

Edward: Sweetness, I am hoping that all is well on the job and the Boss is chilly. Smooch you up, and down!

Mindy: Thank you for checking on me. Smooch you. Happy day!

Mindy: Kiss you!!!

From: Edward
To: Mindy
Date: Monday, September 12
Subject: Friday Night ... Yaaaayyy!

Sweet Mindy, again I am in Carly Simon mode ("Anticipation"). I am prepared to realize that we do not really like each other, but feel that we should verify this tragic circumstance. To be sure.

  Please, recline beneath my face, my dear. Oh yes ...
Sweet dreams and kisses all over.
Edward

From: Mindy
To: Edward
Date: Tuesday, September 13
Subject: RE: Friday Night ... Yaaaayyy!

This e-mail from you made my toes curl ... just so you know ... you are beyond adorable, my sweet Edward.
So let's just allow things to simmer in our brains and see what our subconscious cooks up in the next few hours.
The good news is: we are looking at 3 nights together rather than 2 AND we don't have to be quiet, should the situation arise ... but I am also mindful that we can't keep shelling out $$ for hotels at the beach. We will figure it out, dear Edward. It's all good and how wonderful to have choices AND myriad hotels at our disposal!
Jumping in the shower ... more in a few.
Mindy Xoxoxo

Tuesday, September 13 - Phone Texts

Mindy: So excited to see you again ... we'll iron it out. :-)

Edward: I thought I would swing by the adult store and check on a goody or two for us!

Mindy: SO excited about our weekend! Please don't over think it ... no pressure on us ... I am saying these things to you to remind me, of course!

Edward: Be Here Now, be there soon! Will not be soon enough ...

Mindy: Yaaayyy!!! Did you have fun shopping? I want to hear all about it ... just leaving work ... shall I call you from the car?

Edward: No dear, I don't want you talking on the phone while you are driving. I will call after I get home.   :-)

MINDY:

Expectations Revisited

Edward and I have many in-depth conversations around us, the possibility of us, the truth of us, and how we are going to proceed. Neither one of us ever imagined (well, Edward probably did) that we would get along so well on so many levels: physical, spiritual, and emotional. We have such a fun time together and can carry on for hours. We speak the same language.

However, the truth of it is that we live 3.5 hours away and there continues to be some question around our compatibility

153

over the long haul. We both want us to be good together. But reality says that we should keep searching in our own necks of the wood. To this end, we continue (albeit, half-heartedly) on the Dating Site.

Edward's deep end of the pool seems to be teeming with women. My end of the pool seems to be shallow when it comes to available men of interest.

It is a testimony to trust (or insanity) that we both continue to talk like we are in a relationship (but always with the caveat that it may be ending shortly), and yet try to stay open to another person coming into our life. I struggle with this more than Edward, it seems, which doesn't mean that he doesn't care as much. He just has a better grasp on reality and the facts of what is possible. I am prone to living in the land of "worst case scenario," which makes Edward and his "be here now" nature cringe. Together, we are a good balance.

Every time he goes on a first date to meet with someone from the Dating Site my heart stops and my stomach churns. Every time I go on a date, I find myself comparing the unsuspecting soul to Edward, although I try to remain open and willing. It is a huge emotional conundrum.

In the meantime, knowing that this will be our "real, last physical meeting" we make plans to spend another weekend mid-way on the map to see if we really like each other as much as we think we do. Or something like that. The plan is to meet in Ashland, for three nights this time, taking a chance on turning into a pool of melted love butter!

> From: Mindy
> To: Edward

Date: Tuesday, September 13
Subject: RE: Reservation Confirmation for September 16

Hooray for us!!!!!!
Smooch you, baby ... so excited to see/feel you again!
Mindy
Xoxoxox

From: Mindy
To: Edward
Date: Tuesday, September 13
Subject: Mindy's Vision

Dear Edward,
Several months ago I sat down and wrote my two-year vision for my life, what would transpire and result two years from the time I wrote it. I am attaching that for you. I am thinking you might find it interesting. It is so exciting to be manifesting this vision ... creating intention is a powerful thing, which you well know.
Kisses, Mindy

MINDY'S VISION MAP

I happily anticipate my yearly, month-long visit to SOUKYA in Southern India. I miss my friends and the holistic emotional, spiritual and physical healing I gain from my time there. Financial independence allows me to travel when and where I choose, in luxurious fashion, and my annual trip to Soukya is my favorite destination each year. It is an effortless journey that keeps me grounded, serene and intensely happy.

My work with others also fulfills me on all of these levels. I live every day with an attitude of gratitude and the expectation of continued abundance. As each day unfolds, I marvel at the wonder and grace that surrounds me with love.

My partner fulfills, encourages and excites me to do and be better. The co-creation of our life together also enhances our separate ability to serve others. We are an exciting force for good and change in our and others' lives. We live a healthy, thoughtful and intentional life, both individually and together.

My ability to create and manage my income from anywhere enables me to live where my heart, mind and body needs to be to thrive: sun, the sound and view of water, and sandy beaches for daily walking. Saltwater nurtures my spirit and body. I am healthy and whole and becoming more so every day. I share this exciting healthy sober lifestyle with my partner. I am blessed beyond measure.

I am valued, trusted and sought out for my organizational intuitive abilities and skills. I write and speak about creating a culture of wholeness and financial abundance. I create and maintain new ventures and adventures with a trusted team of co-creators. My vision is limitless, effortless and achieved on a daily basis. I can smell the salt air. I can feel my toes wiggling in the sand. I can feel my heart expanding. I gleefully hold hands with my partner in life and joyful co-creation. I lean into his strength and kindness. Wealth-building comes naturally to me. I serve others and, in doing so, have created the amazing life I now experience. My gifts are many and are recognized and rewarded financially by others. I serve from my heart. I am a catalyst for good. I create an "environment of retirement" for my clients.

I write, speak, encourage and advise on creating successful visions. I enable my clients to move to their next higher good, moving ever forward in faith and trust. I have an exhilarating life and I readily share it with others. I am surrounded by friends and supportive, like-minded teachers of every kind. I am the jumping-off point for others to achieve their highest good. I love my life and what I accomplish, effortlessly, every day! Miracles abound as I daily put into motion the reason why I am here.

I now enjoy the perfect balance of doing and being. I am surrounded by amazingly creative and integrity-filled people, who encourage and support my vision and goals. My faith is limitless. I anticipate the good. Wonders never cease.

I sigh with contentment as I watch the sun gradually set after another amazing day with my life partner. The warm tide laps at my toes. I am intensely happy, healthy and in love. I value my life and what I can offer to others.

I have plenty of time to do what I love and the health and wherewithal to travel whenever I want.

Wednesday, September 14 - Phone Texts

Mindy: Thinking about this weekend makes me weak in the knees and squirmy all over ... mmmmm. Sweet Edward!

Edward: If you think you are weak and squirmy now, wait until I get a hold on you!

Thursday, September 15 - Phone Texts

Mindy: Exciting happenings on the horizon ... get to see my sweetie soon. Did some culling of the Roundup site last night.

Edward: I'm excited to see my sweetie again. Curious to

hear about your site culling. Have a good day dear!

Mindy: Heading into work … girding my loins …

Edward: Wish I was there to help you gird, but that would probably just slow things down.

Mindy: Trying to get organized to leave tomorrow. Mtg w/ client starts @ 1:30 … will probably take 2-3 hours then I will hit the road and head to you. ;-)

Edward: Good plan. Sounds like we will both arrive about the same time. I am so looking to spoon up with you girl! After the nibble fest! :-p

Friday, September 16 – Phone Texts
Mindy: Good morning … see you in a few.   :-)

Mindy: Smooch you!

Edward: I will see your excited and raise you an ecstatic! Soon …

Mindy: Yaaayyy us!!

Edward: I sure am glad you thought of this girl.

Mindy: I'm here!

CHAPTER 21

Second Meeting
9/17/11 – 9/19/11
Overnight Suites
Ashland, VA

EDWARD:

This is our second "One Visit Theory"

I took off work at lunch time to get an early start on the journey to visit Mindy in Ashland. Another mission to accomplish on the way is to stop back by Public Health and get the results of my STD tests. As I had expected, I was found to be healthy and socially acceptable and safe to play with. Excellent ... we no longer need to use the party favors the nurse gave me when I was there last!

As a woman who has had to rely on her own devices (double entendre intended) for several years, Mindy has a couple sex toys for her satisfaction. At least she can alleviate the hormonally driven urges so she can get to sleep at night. (It is nice to know that women are affected that way, much the same as men.) I have suggested that we go shopping for adult toys for us to share in our explorations.

I expect that Ashland, being a college town, would have at least one adult novelty store. We go online in search of info about adult toys in this neck of the woods. The good old Internet is as diverse and misdirecting as usual. Three or four links are for online businesses only, not the help we need. A couple of business names/numbers are in the list but when we call the phone numbers, we learn that they have been disconnected. There is one listing left and it is actually in

Ashland, not Richmond twenty miles down the road. When we call that number, we don't get an answer but we also don't get a "been disconnected" message. It is late Saturday afternoon, and seems like appropriate time for such a business to be operational. Maybe they were just too busy helping customers to answer the phone. So we decide to go for a ride, do a little adult toy shopping and then get some supper before returning to our room to check our new purchases.

MINDY:
Sex Toys

Prior to our first meeting, Edward mentioned the opportunity of using sex toys and encouraged me to bring mine. So this rendezvous we are planning on shopping for toys together. I am throwing caution (and comfort) to the wind to fully embrace this new adventure with my training wheels instructor, Mr. Edward.

To this end, we go online in our hotel room and look for sex shops. You would think that a college town would be fraught with such places. Not so much. Online we look for "Adult Toys." Most sites are for mail order only and we don't have that kind of time. We want the adventure of shopping together complete with conversations, explanations and exclamations!

We find one and only one likely candidate: "Tina's Toys". However, no one answers the phone when we call. So we decide to drive by and stop in to see what Tina has going on. Imagine our surprise when we discover that Tina's toys are poodles! Yes, Tina is a breeder of toy poodles. She sells "adult toys." But, alas, not the kind we are looking for. We are forced to return to our room and fend for ourselves, with ourselves. Poor babies ... not. Truly lucky ducks ... yes!

EDWARD:

On our first visit, we had managed to leave the room long enough to get some of the breakfast available as part of our accommodations. On this, our second visit, Mindy stays in the room while I use my "chipmunk shorts" to procure breakfast. These are cargo shorts, complete with large pockets on the outside of the leg. There's plenty of room for apples, bananas, yogurt and faux cheese Danish. Two cups of coffee occupy my hands and viola, we have our morning meal!

Once again, I find myself in the realm of unknowingly trying to poison my sweetie … she doesn't care for bananas and she's allergic to apples. "Note to Self: Add apples to the No-No list with peanuts." But the yogurt and Danish are acceptable and sufficient so we don't fall over from lack of nourishment.

Monday, September 19 - Phone Texts

Mindy: My dear sweet Edward … just arrived home. Thank YOU for a most exceptional weekend … I am agog. :-D at the wonderment of us. Hope all is well with your dad. I love my beautiful pin (Sterling and Amber Rose) and I love you. Thank you for your amazing self. Mindy.

Edward: Thank you dear, for sharing your sweet self with me. Is it possible that we still do not really like each other? Excellent weekend!

Mindy: Good night, sweet Edward. Thank you for a most amazing weekend …

Edward: Sweet dreams, my dear. We are our pleasure …

oh darn. :-*

Tuesday, September 20 - Phone Texts

Edward: Good morning, sweetness! Have a most excellent day!

Mindy: And to you, my sweets! Back to reality…

Mindy: Edward!! I miss our bliss. :-)

Edward: Missin' blissin' with my lady. :-(

Friday, September 23 - Phone Texts

Edward: Hey Mindy! What's for supper, girl?

Mindy: I've got your supper right here! :-D

Mindy: Would like to get naughty with you, my sweets. Two weeks. Good to have time to heal between bouts-o-love. ;-)

Edward: Maybe I could kiss it and make it better. Or is that how the need to heal gets started?

Mindy: Goodnight love baby! I am feeling especially squirmy for you. Mmmmmmm ... sweet dreams of you. :-P

From: Mindy
To: Edward

Date: Wednesday, September 28
Subject: Thought for the Day

Dear Edward,
Everything is perfectly perfect. We are each here for
the other; we agreed to be so many lifetimes ago. It has
definitely been worth the wait, my sweets.
Mindy

Wednesday, September 28 - Phone Texts

Mindy: Yayyy you! Yayyy me! Yayyy us!!! Methinks the
universe is trying to make a major point and I am just not
seeing it. In the meantime, it is so painful. You, love, are
my balm. Mmmmm…

Edward: I am hoping to be able to make the pain go
away. Kiss you up and down, make it mo' betta! Smooch
you!

Mindy: Shall I arrive tomorrow for toy shopping after
you get home from work? I can entertain myself Friday
while you are at work. It will give us one more night.

Edward: Another night sounds wonderful, dear! Toys,
play, rest … great combo!

Mindy: Goodnight, love. Thanks for the scintillating
chat. We'll figure it out. Smooch you soon!

CHAPTER 22

Third Meeting
9/29/11 – 10/2/11
Smithfield, VA

EDWARD:

For our third "One Visit Theory," I booked a room at a motel for privacy, just around the corner from the house where I am renting a room. Mindy leaves work at lunch time on Thursday and drives on down, the last third of the journey being through the country, a most pleasant ride. The timing of her travel is pretty well coordinated with my schedule and I meet her at the motel after my work day. We get settled in, have some dinner and cuddle up together.

The next day, Friday, I go to work at my normal early time. Mindy sleeps in and then amuses herself around town with window shopping, a bit of lunch and a walk in the local park. This evening we go to a small local restaurant, have a pleasant meal and then embark on a bit of shopping for our mutual enjoyment. We go to the adult toy store in a nearby city, the store we had been looking for in Ashland but did not find.

The merchant is a non-chain movie rental business. They have all the standard public offerings, suitable for the entire family. In the back corner, visually shielded from the front store area by a partition, is the entrance to Adult World. They have quite a variety of doo-dads and gee-gaws. They have stuff I don't know what you do with. But they also have an extensive array of toys designed to help you and your dear friend derive the most pleasure within the vessel of our bodies, the excellent and exotic bodies that contain our souls. If we aren't supposed to enjoy ourselves, we wouldn't be designed to provide and perceive so much pleasure. And I mean in all aspects of the words, mental, physical, and spiritual.

The two young women at the register welcome us and ask to see our ID's, making sure we are of age to decide about adult matters. The store is large, clean and brightly lit. So many colors, sizes and shapes.

Mindy has been a solo person for seven years. But having a physique, mind, and attitude that still relishes pleasure, she has a couple toys already. She is not unaware of these things. I am thrilled, I am complimented that she is brave and trusting me enough to be comfortable going with me to shop for adult toys. (These toys are not poodles, though that reminds me of an album title … "Let Me Play with Your Poodle" by Marcia Ball). And so, the sweet spirit, Mindy, and I wander about, looking, discussing, and determining what we would like to experiment with, what we would like to help us play with each other. Questions and laughter are shared, decisions are made, merchandise is paid for and we are on our way … onward, into the future!

Saturday morning the chipmunk shorts and I procure breakfast. Midday we drive to Norfolk and enjoy lunch at a long time favorite restaurant of mine. They make, and we devour, a killer Greek salad. Then we go to MacArthur Mall and do a little shopping. I'm looking for some Hawaiian shirts (for dancing comfort) and a new pair of shoes for dancing the Carolina Shag. We find both kinds of merchandise and return to our country love nest, content to wrap ourselves around each other and steep, basking in the glow of us. For people that are not the right folks for each other, we sure do like each other a great deal and get along so fine!

MINDY:
Sex Toys Revisited

Finally! We are on Edward's home turf and he knows where the sex shop is. This is not to say that he spends a lot of time in such places. Or so he says.

It is a Friday night and we casually saunter into a shop that is your basic family video rental in the front section to cover for the adult shopping in the back. The two tatted girls behind the counter are barely pushing 18 years old. They look at us somewhat askance (or is that horror?!) as we stroll through and to the adult section in the back. I think I giggled, which probably didn't help matters. I can only imagine how the sight of people our age buying sex toys must appear to these young women. I feel somewhat pathetic and tawdry. And excited by my brazenness.

The adult section is huge! We are like kids in a candy store! We are back there for so long that one of the girls approaches us to inquire if we need any help. "No, we're good." Just perusing, speculating and imagining. If a couple has any qualms about discussing sexual matters, shopping together in an adult paraphernalia store is a great way to overcome them: "What do you think this is for?" "Would you like to try this?" "How would this feel?" It opens the doors to many conversations about pleasing, pleasure and parameters. It is a wonderful opportunity to gain clarity around your partner's wishes and boundaries.

We take our selections and head proudly to the counter up

front. We are politely asked if we need batteries. I look at Edward. He shakes his head no, we have batteries at home. We take our purchases, head across the parking lot to the car and burst into laughter. We are so bad.

From: Mindy
To: Edward
Date: Sunday, October 2
Subject: Pictures:

We keep forgetting to take them! You looked especially handsome in your yellow shirt! I guess dim hotel rooms aren't the best light for photo oops!

From: Edward
To: Mindy
Date: Sunday, October 02
Subject: Re: Pictures:

After I got home, I also remembered that we forgot photos. We need to find a cabana boy to take with us, for those photo ops. What do you think?

From: Mindy
To: Edward
Date: Sunday, October 2
Subject: Re: Pictures:

Mmmmmm ... YOU are my cabana boy. ;-)

From: Edward
To: Mindy
Date: Sunday, October 2
Subject: Re: Pictures:

I just need to tighten up on the photo taking. I will try to do better. Somehow, I keep getting discrackted. Not sure how ...

From: Mindy
To: Edward
Date: Sunday, October 2
Subject: Re: Pictures:

Smooch you and your slacker ways, my sweets!

From: Edward
To: Mindy
Date: Sunday, October 2
Subject: Slacken My Shoes

Thank you for still liking such a slacker. I'm wearing my new shoes in my room at the house, trying to loosen them down. I've got a lot of work to do to have them comfy by next week for dancing. See what I can do. In the mean time, smooch you all over. ;-b :-* Apparently, I'm so discrackted I can't kiss straight...

From: Mindy
To: Edward

Date: Sunday, October 2
Subject: RE: Tight things

How do the shoes feel so far? If they are tight anywhere you can wear thicker socks to stretch them out a bit. Remember when I was tight and you had to put a sock on it?!

From: Edward
To: Mindy
Date: Sunday, October 2
Subject: Re: Tight things

Shoes are a bit up tense but doing alright. I am wearing the yellow socks for stretchage as well as foot protection. I remember when you were tight ... that was this morning. My memory is longer than other parts of me. I remember you asking me to put a sock on it, and then letting me slide (arr arr). Sweetness, are you ready to call me? I'm about ready to go to bed. I need to rest up. I've got a long weekend ahead of me and need to get energized.

EDWARD:

In phone conversation, Mindy and I decide to visit again, (where will this end?) this time at her home.

From: Mindy
To: Edward
Date: Monday, October 3
Subject: Weekend shopping list

- What kind of stuff do you need for your coffee?? I have Splenda sweetener and also real sugar.
- What kind of creamer?
- Snacks?
- Anything else you need on hand?

You will be arriving in the evening on Friday so I am getting our Saturday breakfast in order so we can sleep in AND still get to our appt in DC on time.

From: Edward
To: Mindy
Date: Monday, October 3
Subject: Re: Weekend shopping list

Hello Sweet,

In my coffee, I like a short sugar and milk or cream. I can bring creamer. For breakfast, I usually have plain yogurt with some cereal on top and a splash of my coffee creamer (I use heavy whipping cream ... a personal treat since I use little of it at once), mix it all up and it's yummy. I can bring cereal. What is on your mind for breakfast? I am open to suggestion. Snacks, I don't do much of, but you know I like having a little something around for whenever. I can bring nuts and dried fruit for that. Any other food supplies, we can walk to the store and pick up. As to hands, I want/ need you in and on them (sit on my hand little girl).

Is there anything in particular that you want me to bring from my collection of stuff? Music? How many pair of shoes and pants do I need?

Bringing the plan together, yeah baby!!

From: Mindy
To: Edward
Date: Monday, October 3
Subject: RE: Weekend shopping list

Mmmmm … sit on your hand, indeed.
I know how you love to plan in advance so…
- Bring any snacks you like but know that you don't have to bring a ton of stuff as I live close to a grocery store.
- Def bring music as my only source is the boom box … alarming as that might be. Not even sure if my TV will be working. But will try and get that figured out today after the hvac debacle as it looks like they won't be installing today.
- Just bring jeans and a couple of shirts. Undies, if you're so inclined. Sunday is the pig roast and dance so whatever you think for that.

From: Mindy
To: Edward
Date: Wednesday, October 5
Subject: RE: Weekend shopping list

Love,
What is a "short sugar"?

From: Edward
To: Mindy
Date: Thursday, October 6
Subject: Re: Weekend shopping list

Good morning dear,

That just means a short teaspoon of sugar ... 2/3 of a spoon. I understand how that was not so clear. I will strive to provide clarity of mind with you when I arrive, and thru the weekend, my Chef of Love!! I like cooking with you!

From: Mindy
To: Edward
Date: Thursday, October 6
Subject: Re: Weekend shopping list

Love,
I am your short sugar! ;-)

CHAPTER 23

Fourth Meeting
10/7/11 – 10/10/11
Mindy's House

MINDY:

I am organized by nature. I can't move from Point A to Point B without having my ducks in a row. While I don't like to think of myself as an emotionally plodding person, I am a pretty low scorer on the spontaneity scale. That is why I relish spending time with folks who have this gift. Even though I am not adept at thinking things up, I am always willing to go along for the adventure. Edward was just such an adventure.

Over the years, I have helped others get organized in their thoughts, writing, work and homes. I love pulling a string through other's confusion. And I look to others to help me with mine. It is always difficult to sort one's own stuff. And it is something of a gift to be aware of that.

About 5 years ago, I downsized myself from a 3-story townhome into a much smaller condo. I was ready to trade suburbia for more urban energy. The process of downsizing is mentally clarifying, emotionally healing and physically freeing. I also believe that opening up space in our lives allows new and wondrous things to enter.

It only made sense to help Edward make sense of his cluttered surroundings. Over his lifetime he has accumulated even more lifetimes of stuff, relying on storage units to house his things while he is in transition. Storage units are the result of a culture that thinks it needs more stuff than it really does. Temporarily, it is a great idea; as a long-term solution, it is expensive and smacks of denial. It is difficult to move on in life when one is tethered to old belongings and emotions.

EDWARD:

One of the myriad of topics Mindy and I have discussed is downsizing one's collection of belongings. In her younger youth, she had a consulting business as a personal organizer. It seemed that a majority of that business centers on getting people to actually let go of masses of personal property, especially when it is not being utilized regularly.

A little over a year ago I moved out of my long time home/house in Norfolk because I could no longer afford it. In so doing, I had to deal with what can be accumulated in twenty-four years. The attic was sixteen feet by thirty feet, three feet deep from end to end, with a small trail down the middle. The two car, un-garage had become a repository for so much booty retrieved from addition/renovation jobs. "I don't know what I need it for but it's too good to throw away."

When my wife and I got married, we each had a house full of the necessary household parts. We had blended and culled that assortment but still had a house full, plus. In addition to that, both of her parents and my mother were deceased and each passing had left us with more worldly goods. My house had become more a storage unit than a functional residence.

In moving out of the house in Norfolk, I discarded things that were actually trash (after all these years.) Anything with utility left in it that I didn't want to retain, went to friends or thrift/charity stores. I would much rather give it away if it can still be used. I disposed of two-thirds of the cubic feet and tonnage of my collective stuff. Even so, I ended up with two storage units in Norfolk, each ten by twenty, chock full from top to bottom. What I needed to outfit my room went to Smithfield. I did find it refreshing and liberating to let go of so much stuff. Less to keep track of, search through, and move.

Our fourth "One Visit Theory" was my traveling to stay with Mindy in her home. She had shared photos of her lovely town home shortly after we got acquainted. I am even more favorably impressed when I saw it in person. It is the exemplification of her "downsizing" conversations and life style. Uncluttered, organized, functional, and most attractive. Not really a large surprise to find this as part of the world of this most attractive woman who chose not to disappear from my view. Thank you Ms. Mindy!

> From: Edward
> To: Mindy
> Date: Thursday, October 13
> Subject: Our Cute Selves

Mindy!!

Sweetheart, let's just go ahead and plan to get together the weekend of 21, 22, 23.

I started looking in the newspaper for an apartment or a house (preferably) to rent. If I do that and can use my stuff, I can get rid of one storage unit, at least. Then you could visit me and we can stay at my place, instead of spending money for a hotel. Or I visit you at your house. Less money spent, overall.

Hug you up. Kiss you gently all over. Yummeau!! . . . Edward

From: Mindy
To: Edward
Date: Thursday, October 13
Subject: RE: Our Cute Selves

Baby!!

Yaaayyy us for seeing each other again, SOON. Shall we meet in Ashland Friday night (10/21)? That way we will have all day Saturday and some of Sunday to spend together at "our" hotel ☺ And our fav BBQ place close by. Maybe there is something going on at the college that would be fun to do ... other than us doing us, of course!

Fun to think about you getting out of your current digs and into a more peaceful/supportive environment. You don't need a BIG place ... just SOME place to call home and be yourself.

Love you. Smooch you.

Mindy

MINDY:

From Time To Time

My head gets out of sync with my heart and I panic. For all my talk about living in the moment and not caring where "the tides take us," I truly do want a relationship that will last. And I wonder if I am just fooling myself into thinking that it is possible with Edward.

Saturday, October 15 - Phone Texts

Mindy: My heart is heavy.

Edward: Why is your heart heavy dear? Have you been thinking about the illogic of us together? I understand and it makes me sad as well. I try not to think about it. How's that for good honest philosophy and practice?

Mindy: I never expected to fall so in love with you ... and I can't be the person you want me to be.

Edward: I expected to like you. I didn't expect to like you so much. And I didn't expect to fall in love so quickly. How did that happen?

Mindy: Yes ... who knew? Love you, too. I remember exactly how I felt when we agreed to do this ... even if it ended up hurting in the end our meeting and loving would be more than worth it. And it has been.

Wednesday, October 19 - Phone Texts
Edward: Mindy girl! I am so looking to kiss you all over!

Mindy: I am totally squirmified. :-D

Edward: Love you, dear! Smooch you soon. :-*

Mindy: Love you!

Thursday, October 20 - Phone Texts
Mindy: Hi baby ... just got to work. Girding my loins ... wish I was girding you ... soon!!

Edward: I'll help gird you girl!

Mindy: Can you believe that we first met hardly knowing anything about each other or if we were serial killers or stalkers ... and spent such an amazing soul-stretching 3 days and nights ... the reality of it blows me away ... we really were so brave ... both of us!

Edward: It was all your doing, dear brave girl. You are the blurter. I am simply the blurtee.

Mindy: Good night, love. It struck me tonight that I no longer worry about if we will still like each other when next we meet. Sweet dreams. Love you. Soon smooch!!

Edward: I am so relieved that we finally resolved that whole "liking each other" question. Good night, dear. Kisses!

Friday, October 21 - Phone Texts

Mindy: Woke up early ... got lots to do ... excited to see you in a few ... that is my morning poem for you!

Edward: I'm getting packed so I am able to get underway directly from work. Good morning, sweetness!!

Mindy: Leaving now ... see you soon!!

Edward: Go girl! Or better yet, come on down!

Mindy: Sorry for all the texts ... you must be busy! Arrived and changed our room from a regular king to a king suite AND saved us $20 / night ... WTF??!! Getting settled in. Drive safe. Smooch you!

Edward: Great job dear! I am on my way. Be there in a few. :-)

Mindy: Room 209. :-P

Mindy: Are you here yet??

Edward: Ten more minutes, dear. Well, maybe an hour and ten minutes. Moving to you as quickly as I can, sweets!

CHAPTER 24

Fifth Meeting
10/21/11 – 10/23/11
Overnight Suites
Ashland, VA

MINDY:
Health

I try to take care of myself. At first, this was due to an inbred pride of looking good/better/best than anyone else. Over the years it has turned into more of a concern for aging in the best way possible.

In 1999, armed with a litany of woes, I met a homeopathic physician who assured me homeopathy could help with my allergies, depression, premenopausal symptoms and the "feeling less than" that comes with an unexpected divorce. I was cautioned that the cure would take time; that it took many years for me to get in the shape I was in. In true Type-A fashion I blurted, "But how can I make this happen more quickly?!" The good doctor's response was that I could go to India and be immersed in holistic modalities at his clinic.

And, in my heart of hearts, I knew that I should do this. It was that internal voice that is sometimes heard over the everyday garble in my brain. Two months later, after a lengthy and arduous flight, I land in Bangalore, India and begin my detoxification and healing process.

Holistic medicine has changed my life. I no longer rely on allopathic medications that, eventually, just result in the need of more medications to quash the side effects of the original medications. I search for solutions that deal with the underlying disease, not just the symptoms.

This isn't to say I always lead a disciplined and healthy lifestyle! I love buttered popcorn and all manner of ice-cream and I really don't like to exercise all that much. I tend to worry and ruminate. But I also know what to do to counter these personality traits: I detox, I do yoga, I stretch and focus on flexibility and, all things considered, have managed to live the past 60 years in a pretty healthy fashion.

I am in great hopes that the next 60 years will be just as fun and fruitful.

EDWARD:
"One Visit Theory" #5
Health

As part of my father's Army career, we were in Germany from my ages of five through eight. Consequently, I did not see television until we came back to the U.S. Even then, television was not a large part of my life. After the school work was done, most time was spent outdoors playing with friends. We amused ourselves with physical activities.

In high school, freshman year, I got excited about football and went out for the junior varsity team. While the coach was telling us to separate into groups with the linemen over here and the back field over there, I was busy running my mouth to a buddy. Out of that, I found my scrawny self with the linemen instead of with the back fielders where I had envisioned myself in glory. I was too embarrassed to tell on myself so I attempted to become a lineman. I made the team, sat out the first game and broke my arm in practice the next day. I didn't realize it until later but that was the best thing that could have happened to my football career. My knees have been forever grateful.

Then I allowed a buddy to suck me into the track team my sophomore and junior years. There, I ran a poor mile and acquired no glory, but I survived.

The only sport that I did well, the only sport I really enjoyed, was swimming. That was a natural fit and I did that the summers before junior and senior years. That gave me small vestiges of glory, though no enhanced status at the high school.

Through my various experiences growing up, I've been fortunate to be healthy for the most part. I took it for granted until I hit my twenties. Then, as part of my expanding awareness of the world and events around me, I started paying attention to my own health. I read a few books, learned about vitamins and supplements and started adding them to my daily diet. At that time, I had no concept of twenty, thirty, forty years later … and here we are.

I maintained my slender high school build until I was thirty-five and started working in the office, estimating, instead of working with my carpenter's tools on the job. Then the sedentary lifestyle started making my scales read heavier. Later, with the various emotions surrounding my wife's illness, I sought solace in food and turned into a butterball, not attractive or healthy.

Shortly before I started learning to dance the Carolina Shag, I decided to do something to improve the condition my condition was in, and I actually did it. The dancing has helped and is the most fun form of exercise for me. There is still room for improvement but I am pleased to see progress.

There are the various tests that are recommended as we reach new stages of our lives and I have finally gotten around to them. The world of modern medicine is improving as we speak. They know so much more now than even yesterday. But it is important for you to be your own advocate, learn about your own health and speak up for yourself when seeing a doctor. And remember, they don't know everything and there are different approaches. My GP prescribed a steroid cream for a small burn that did not want to heal. I applied the steroid for a year and in fact, the unhappy place on my skin got larger, not smaller or better. My sweetheart, Ms. Mindy, suggested that I try a homeopathic medicine. My burn is finally healing.

We did not get an owner's manual with these bodies, so we are kind of on our own, but it's worth the effort to find out what shape we are in and how to maintain it as best possible. I don't care how many dollars you have in the bank. If you don't feel well in your body, it's tough to enjoy anything, and that makes it difficult to feel well within your mind and your spirit.

Please do what you can to go forth, prosper and be healthy, so that you can Live, Learn, Laugh, Love!

Sunday, October 23 – Phone Texts

Mindy: Just got home. Going to take a nap. Thank you for the amazing weekend ... even if you did wreck my hip. =-O Love you, sweetpea!

Edward: Love you dear. Thank you for a wonderful weekend! Can I kiss your hip and make it better? :-*

Monday, October 24 – Phone Texts

Mindy: I need your dad's walker... :-D

Tuesday, October 25 – Phone Texts

Mindy: What's for lunch, baby?

Edward: Baby! A hard salami and provolone roll up. How about you, sweets?

Mindy: Bring your hard salami over here! :-P.

Edward: Shall I bring the walker with me as well?

Mindy: Good to hear your voice before I head to bed. Sleep tight, Mr. Lovepants!!

Thursday, October 27 – Phone Texts

Mindy: How is your perky friend? I miss him. ;-)

Edward: Our perky friend is wondering where you are. He misses you and wants to be close again, several times.

Wednesday, November 2 – Phone Texts

Mindy: What's for lunch?

Edward: A pepperoni and gruyere rollup. Do you have any suggestions for dessert? :-D

Mindy: Me

Edward: Excellent answer. I was hoping you would think of you. I'll start with a double helping, followed by seconds ... nap ... dessert ... repeat ... and that's just to warm up. Later I'll get serious ... Kiss you sweetheart, Love you!

Mindy: Yummers ... warm me up, sweets! SO looking forward to gnoshing and napping with you ... mmmmm Edward: Yumm you, gnoshing and gnapping ... soon my sweetness. Smooches!

Thursday, November 3 – Phone Texts

Mindy: Hi baby ... running around pulling my chit together for tomorrow ... haven't even begun to pack! So happy to see you soon!!!

Edward: Mindy girl! I'm collecting my chit too. Getting ready to see my baby!

Mindy: Goodnight sweets ... this time tomorrow night we shall be entwined ... aaahhhhh!

Edward: Sweetness! I call dibs on being the big spoon first. Kiss you soon! Good night dear.

Friday, November 4 – Phone Texts

Mindy: Thinking about melting into you ... mmmmm

Edward: I am so into melting with my Mindy! Hug and kiss you soon my dear!

CHAPTER 25

Sixth Meeting
11/4/11 -11/6/11
Overnight Suites
Ashland, VA

EDWARD:

Our sixth "One Visit Theory"

We actually get ourselves out of our room a couple times this weekend. The "chipmunk shorts" come in handy for breakfasts. Saturday afternoon we make it out to our new favorite barbecue place. Then we decide to go for a ride in the country in search of a bit of history that my genealogically-inclined cousin has suggested. We visit the Hanover Tavern, one of the few surviving Colonial Era taverns in the United States. It has hosted such historic figures as George Washington, Lord Cornwallis and the Marquis de Lafayette.

VISION MAP

Since Mindy and I seem to be having difficulty with our plans "to be/not to be" together, she suggests that we make vision maps during this visit. She brings many magazines as source material, poster board, scissors and paste sticks. Seems to be all the supplies we will need to help find a vision.

My perception of a vision map is a sort of "stream-of-consciousness" cut and paste picture/poster that conveys our subliminal and conscious desires to the "universe." This helps the universe to send these things our way, or send us in the direction of these things. Superstition lite, but I can go with it.

Can't hurt, might help. Let's do it!

After our visit to Hanover Tavern Saturday afternoon, we choose to do our vision maps. We each grab some magazines and start perusing, cutting out random pictures, words and phrases. You collect those pieces that move you in some way. It is helpful to put a time limit on the collection end of the project. Then you paste different items to your poster board, here and there. Try a little lay-out before you get into the paste.

Mindy and I are working in proximity but we are not working together. Each person's map is to reflect themselves, not someone else. We finish our pasting and inspect our works, our visions. Interestingly enough, we have each chosen a picture of "her feet atop his feet." It is the sort of thing that you might do early on in learning to dance at home on soft carpet. It is something that Mindy and I have done, standing that way, hugging and kissing. The "feet on feet" are bottom center on both maps. There is one striking difference though. They are the same picture but Mindy has left the legs half way up the shins. For some reason that escapes me, even now, I have cut the legs a good bit shorter and that makes them look somewhat odd. Boy, do I have vision. Spread around the rest of the board are words of health, hope, pleasure and desire. There are pictures of beautiful locales, items and people. My favorite is a picture of a loving couple on a grassy hillside in the sun, smiling at each other and holding hands. The angle of the picture puts the sun just above and between their heads, somewhat obscuring their faces. After we have viewed, discussed and admired our vision maps, Mindy tells me that my loving couple appears to be lesbians. I was just seeing a loving couple. Boy, do I have vision!

MINDY:
VISION MAP

I have been creating vision maps for many years. I suppose you could say I am hyper-focused on my future and what it holds. I do tend to struggle with faith, trusting that life will proceed as it is supposed to. I like to feel prepared … or at least live under the illusion of being somewhat prepared.

Vision maps are a way to uncover and expose "what's next." They are always amazing, surprising and life-affirming. And all you need is a piece of poster board, a few old magazines, a pair of scissors and a glue stick.

When Edward (who has been endlessly amenable to these rituals of mine) and I meet to do our vision maps, the question in our minds was "what's next in our lives, not as a couple but as individuals?"

We sit at a table, armed with our magazines and scissors. For about 30 minutes, we cut out any pictures or words/phrases that resonate with us. There is no thinking of a theme; just random words and pictures that catch our attention and spoke to us. (It helps to use magazines that will have the type of words and pictures that you find useful. I always use yoga, health, and travel magazines.)

Once you have your piles of words and pictures you have 30-45 minutes (I have totally made up the time frames for these, but I find if you don't have a time frame, the serendipity gets lost in the over-thinking) to scissor trim, format and glue them to the poster board.

After everyone has their maps completed it's time for "show and tell." One by one, each person stands and explains their vision map and why they chose their particular words and pictures.

Sometimes the results are very random, with a common theme. Sometimes a story develops. The most amazing thing to me is that, time after time, I invariably end up with something on my vision map that I don't even remember putting there ... but it makes perfect sense! It's like your subconscious mind is making the selections for you ... and it all makes perfect sense.

Date the back of your vision map and then place it in a prominent position in your home (I also have one in my office which I created to envision my "perfect client") where you will see it on a regular, if not daily, basis.

You will be amazed by what shows up in your life. After all, Edward showed up in mine!!

Sunday, November 6 – Phone Texts

Edward: Baby!! Thank you for a wonderful weekend! Love you!

Edward: Just finished lunch. Pretty good. Are you home yet? Hugs and kisses!

Mindy: Yes ... made it home ... in something of a daze ... weird to have you close one minute and far away the next ...

Edward: Yes ma'am, strange and lonesome too. :-(

Edward: I've had din ... Have you got supper?

Mindy: I've got your supper right here, love! :-D

Edward: Excellent my dumpling darling. That is what I

was hoping you would say.

Mindy: Heading to bed. Sweet dreams, love. Thank you for the great weekend. Seems like forever until the next one.

Edward: Sweetpea, Right behind you (I wish) on the way to bed. Thank you for our great weekend. Sweet dreams. Love you!

Monday, November 7 – Phone Texts

Edward: Good morning sweetheart, our silly friend woke me up 4 times last night looking for you to play with ... darn ... Smooches!

Mindy: Wtf?!! And here I am soooo far away. :-(Have a safe day, sweets! Miss you and your alert friend, too!

Edward: Sweetheart, you have a good and safe day as well. Us silly boys, we miss you dear. Love you!

Mindy: Love my boys! :-P

Mindy: Good God! I feel like a pretzel ... what did you do to me??!!

Edward: I thought I was helping with your exercise program. Is that not how it worked out? Was I working kinks in, instead of out?

Mindy: I understand if you have changed your mind about me coming for Thanksgiving.

Edward: Why would I change my mind about Thanksgiving? Seeing you reminds me to give thanks! :-)

Tuesday, November 8 – Phone Texts
Mindy: I'm pretty sure you shattered the vertebrae in my neck ... but it was totally worth it!

Edward: Dear Mindy, You are such a brave soul and a good sport too!

Wednesday, November 9 – Phone Texts
Mindy: I know you're busy dancing, but just got home and love my card! You are the sweetest man ever and I am one lucky duck to be in love with you ... baby!!

Edward: Sweetpea, Just a love card for my love baby!

Thursday, November 10 – Phone Texts
Edward: Mindy! What's for supper girl?

Mindy: I totally got yo supper!

Edward: You totally got the supper I want ... I need!!

Mindy: Going to get cute for my baby :-P

Edward: It's tough to get any cuter than you already are, sweets.

Mindy: Ok. My hair is now officially RED. Not sure if I am loving it ... hmmmm.

Edward: Is it red all over?

Mindy: Didn't color everywhere, my dear perverted lover...

Edward: I wasn't asking if the carpet matches the drapes, dear, but I appreciate your interpretation!   :-)

Friday, November 11 – Phone Texts

Edward: Baby! Come climb in the bed and play with me!

Mindy: Oooohhhhh ... would totally love to be playing with you ... mmmmm!

Mindy: Goodnight my love ... I'm climbing into bed with my book ... wish it was you. Hugs and kisses. Sweet dreams!!

Edward: Sweet dreams, dear. Wishin' you were reading me!

Saturday, November 12 – Phone Texts

Mindy: Me being here but knowing you are there makes me so happy ...

Edward: Morning dear. Yes, knowing that my sweetie is out there is comforting, even when she isn't so close.

Monday, November 14 – Phone Texts

Mindy: My busy brain is working on a new plan. ☺
Thanks for keeping me grounded, my sweets!
Edward: You are ever vigilant, in search of a new
adventure! Thank you for sharing with me. :-)

Mindy: Hi baby ... smooch you now and soon in person!

Edward: Smooch you back, and front, repeatedly!!

Wednesday, November 16 – Phone Texts

Mindy: Thinking of you ...

Edward: Thinking of you ... on me. :-)

Thursday, November 17 – Phone Texts

Edward: Kiss you from head to toe, and back again.
Which side do you want me to start on?

Mindy: Kissing all over is totally acceptable. ;-)

Edward: I know, you are just being a good sport and
humoring me, in spite of your disinterest.

Mindy: OK. Sigh ... you know how much I hate kissing
you ...

CHAPTER 26

Seventh Meeting
11/18/11 - 11/20/11
Mindy's House
Reston, VA

EDWARD:
Our seventh "One Visit Theory"

Mindy invites me to visit with her at her home. She wants to share tickets to go see Cirque du Soleil. What I find intriguing is the fact that Mindy bought the tickets long before she met me. She knew she wanted to see this show and she knew she wanted to take someone special. She didn't know who that special person would be. I am pleased that it turned out to be me, for many reasons aside from Cirque. Was it a self-fulfilling projection on her part, an affirmation?

MINDY:
"If You Build It They Will Come!"

Six months prior to meeting Edward, I purchased two tickets to a Cirque du Soleil event in downtown DC that I very much wanted to see … with a special man. My intention was that someone would show up. I took great care in selecting the perfect seats and sent off my payment. Then I promptly forgot about it.

Enter stage left: Edward. We went together and had a wonderful time. It pays to build your "field of dreams" if only to see who shows up. You never know.

CHAPTER 27

Eighth Meeting
11/23/11 -11/27/11   Thanksgiving
Overnight Suites
Smithfield, VA

EDWARD:

Our eighth "One Visit Theory"

Mindy drives down after work on Wednesday and meets me at a motel in Smithfield, where we take up residence for the rest of the week.

Thursday, November 24 - Thanksgiving

I call around, checking on restaurants that are open for Thanksgiving. Not too many folks doing business but I find a few and we choose out of that group. Mindy and I go to Norfolk, pick up my son and we all go to Rancho Oro for lunch! There is certainly more variety available there than the traditional Thanksgiving. Most yummy!

Friday is a regular work day for me so Mindy enjoys sleeping late, being slow and easy, and knocking around Smithfield for the day.

Part of our plan for the weekend is to go dancing. The Colonial Shag Club meets on Saturday evening at a music club in Newport News. There are free shag dance lessons at the beginning of the evening and then it's open for "all dance ... ALL SKATE, ALL SKATE." It was at this location and with these people that I had my first shag dance experience on Valentine's Day. Mindy has some trepidation because she doesn't know anyone. Haven't we all been there? Her fears are quickly dispelled as she is made as welcome and comfortable as I had been, all those months ago.

EDWARD:
The Carolina Shag

If you've seen the Austin Powers movies, you likely have an awareness of the British definition of the word "shag." Apparently, a great many people have seen those movies. Shortly after I started taking shag lessons, I realized that I needed to be cautious when speaking with unfamiliar civilians. I think I offended a couple ladies and almost got myself slapped by talking about "learning to shag." And of course, that conversation begs the question, "How does a person attain your years and not know how to shag?" … "Oh, Behave!" as Austin would say. In self defense, I got in the habit of speaking about "learning to dance the Carolina Shag."

The Carolina Shag was born on the beaches of the Carolinas. It's different from most dances in that the upper body is relatively quiet, non-bouncy or showy. On the other hand, so to speak, the footwork can be quite amazing and wondrous to see done well. It's a slot dance, as if you are dancing on a diving board. The basic step has eight steps, or weight changes, spread over six beats of music. The count is: 1 and 2, 3 and 4, 5, 6. The "and" is a step timed between the beats of music. Women are always right and so, start with their right foot. The men get what's left, so we start with our left foot.

I was lucky enough to fall in with the best instructors in my area. I didn't know that at first but have seen several different instructors since, enough to have an opinion. It's fairly easy to get a grip on the basic step and get started having fun. But after my second lesson, I found I was boring myself because I didn't know enough to mix it up. Fortunately, the third lesson helped me forward and it got better. I was, and am, quite vocal in sharing my thanks with all the lovely and patient ladies for enduring the process and helping me learn how to dance the Carolina Shag. My learning process has had some interruptions. I haven't been able to devote regular time and energy to the dance. Consequently, although I can now mix it up, I'm starting to bore myself again. It's time for more "due diligence" to enhance my happy feet.

MINDY:
My Foray Into The World Of Shag Dancing

My dear sweet Edward has been trying to get me to dance the Carolina Shag since way before I ever met him in person. Edward, you see, has what I call, "dancing feet." The man cannot help himself. He is the Mr. Bo Jangles of the Carolina Shag!

I initially took shag lessons at Edward's recommendation, as a way to meet available men. Little did I know, I would end up actually dancing with Edward!

I was a tad leery of meeting his shag crew at an event where I would know no one. I have a life-long concern regarding looking like a fool. I have no idea why. I don't even KNOW these people! So, I put on my brave big girl outfit and prepared to kinda, sorta dance with these fancy footed folks.

My worry was for naught. Everyone was so inviting and helpful; I immediately felt at home and not at all like the worst dancer in the place (even if I was). Edward is a wonderful dance partner as he's a good lead and can keep me focused. He's very patient and I thoroughly enjoy my first Carolina Shag event. We plan on doing more events as they arise. In the meantime, we each continue to practice with other partners in our own necks of the wood.

Sunday, November 27 – Phone Texts

Mindy: Just got gas before getting on 295. The weekend went by so quickly. ☺ ... but thanks for spending it with lucky girl me. :-)

Edward: Sweetness, thank you for coming down and sharing yourself with me. I am a lucky duck!

Wednesday, November 30 - Phone Texts

Edward: I'm going to rent a house in Hampton. We will have my own place! Yeah!!

Mindy: Wow ... can't imagine being in YOUR bed, for a change ... yeehaw!! When would you plan on moving in? Will it take some time to orchestrate things? Maybe January 1st? Love you, baby!

Mindy: Baby!! Heading into Pilates to get cute for you. :-* Excited to hear all about the house and your plans!

Edward: Mindy!! The cuter you get, the more I will be forced to kiss you, all over. Darn, what a chore.   :-)

Thursday, December 1 – Phone Texts

Edward: I just learned that I have off Friday and Monday for Christmas!

Mindy: WTF?!! What great news!! Whatever shall we do with all that time??? =-O :-P

Edward: We'll have to be brave, and creative. How many different ways can I nibble you from head to toe? We should explore that question!

Mindy: Life is good.

Edward: Life is excellent!

Monday, December 5 – Phone Texts

Edward: Very exciting to be packing up and moving my stuff to the new homestead!

Mindy: Lots to be excited about fo' sho!! I know you're strong and in excellent shape, but be careful with all your moving and lifting of stuff. Go baby!!

Edward: Going forward with care and diligence.

Mindy: Have Pilates @ 6:30. Home around 8. I will text you. :-*

Edward: Getting flexible and strong so we don't break your hip again?

Mindy: My hips only want to be broken by you. :-P

Tuesday, December 6 – Phone Texts

Edward: Sweetpea! Gobble you up girl! Kissing your thither and yons!

Mindy: Baby! I was just going to send you a mushy message ... cool how we are always so in tune with each other!! Love you. Smooch you. Wrap my legs around you! :-P

Friday, December 9 – Phone Texts

Edward: I'm concerned about having the house put together by the time you come to visit. There's a lot of stuff to move and organize.

Mindy: Just set up the queen bed and we are good to go. Focus on getting out of the old house. Stay out of "analysis paralysis" my love. I'll help you figure it out when I get there ... and I'll check the shui of it. :-*

Monday, December 12 – Phone Texts

Mindy: Having lunch with a friend. Since my meeting this afternoon with a different friend moved to yesterday, I'm trying to get a Pilates session in tonight. Gots to get cute for my baby!

Edward: Get down with your cute bad self, girl!

Mindy: Speaking of bad ... what's for supper! :-P

Edward: I started listing something in the way of food

and then realized ... wait a minute. I'm talking about din and you're asking about supper ... You are what's for supper my dear!

Mindy: Haha! Good catch!

Edward: No sweets. You are a great catch, and super supper too!

Thursday, December 22 – Phone Texts

Mindy: Heading home to get my chit together for early departure to your arms tomorrow morning. :-D

Edward: I am so looking forward to cuddling up with you, my dear.

CHAPTER 28

Ninth Meeting
12/23/11 -12/27/11 Christmas
Edward's House
Hampton, VA

EDWARD:

Our ninth "One Visit Theory"

My darling Mindy comes to visit me in my new house in Hampton. It's the Christmas holidays. Mostly we are lazy but one of our topics of conversation is the art of Feng Shui. Mindy has made a copy of an information chart to help me with the basics so I can balance the energy of my surroundings. One critical part of that conversation is how to enhance the Shui o' Love.

We have a wonderful relaxing weekend, and she goes home on Monday. Over the next couple days, we carry on as usual but something seems a little bit off ... can't put my finger on it.

MINDY:

The Shui O' Love

I have a fair-to-middling knowledge of Feng Shui. I'm also a firm believer in the power of intention. For years I've taught my clients that "energy creates energy;" that which we focus on expands. It's all about clarity, function, and flow. In my years as a professional organizer, I saw this become repeatedly apparent in my clients' lives. I've also witnessed it many times in my own.

Over our Christmas meeting, I offer to shui Edward's new rental home. It was immediately obvious that since the back right corner of his house was "missing," in a manner of speaking, so was his relationship corner. I told him this could be remedied by burying something in his yard where the corner of his house should be, perhaps heart-shaped. Perhaps a heart shaped stone or some other love-related item. I thought it would be best to bury it so he wouldn't run into or over it when he mowed the yard.

Another idea: those small pavers (stepping stones) you can make with kits from arts-n-crafts stores. The ones where little kids can decorate a paver stone to place in their yard. The kits come with a form, some sort of material that can be decorated and then hardened and placed in the yard.

We also talk about other areas of his house and how to "bump up" their Feng Shui factor.

In truth, the conversation around bumping up Edward's relationship corner is bittersweet. I can't quite shake the feeling that we are supposed to appreciate our experience together but go our separate ways. My fear of emotional pain is keeping me from fully committing. Our differences seem to become magnified when I am in this frame of mind. I am not afraid of being alone, but I am afraid of hurting. Will it hurt less if I nip it in the bud?

EDWARD:

Wednesday, December 28

We are speaking on the phone on Wednesday evening, and Mindy tells me that she realizes we are not the folks for each other on a long term. Although we enjoy, like and love each other, we have known from the beginning that we weren't necessarily traveling on concurrent paths. We still reside 200 miles apart and are each held in our current zip codes by the demands of career, as well as the different directions of our lives.

A goodly part of our connection is due to having shared many of the same experiences, traveling in similar circles in our younger youth. I am still emotionally involved in that spirit and energy. Good, bad, or indifferent, I look forward to revisiting. Also, I would like for my partner to go there with me. Mindy can't join me there. Suspecting, or knowing this for a while doesn't make it any easier to face or hurt any less. I have been blissfully encamped in Egypt, living beside Denial. Now I'm drowning in harsh reality. It's my own voluntary blindness that has allowed us to arrive at this place. Yet, I can't imagine making any different decisions along the way.

We sadly agree that we are no longer going steady. She's being the adult and saying these things out loud … I've been waiting for this shoe to drop, wondering when these words would be spoken. Emotionally, it's not what I want to hear or how I want it to be. Logically, I concur that it's wisest for us to travel in our solo directions. We are still dear friends.

MINDY:

I am afraid. I am ruled by the fear that lives between my ears. For nearly 60 years I have struggled to live in trust and believe that the best shall prevail. It's a constant challenge to see myself as enough.

On the other hand, I am also afraid that I will miss an opportunity to be someone better. Past hurts have made me skeptical. My default is to doubt people, places and things. For years I have protected myself against the emotional bogeymen I see lurking behind every corner. It is exhausting to tote this protective armor everywhere I go.

But I am afraid. And it is this fear that leads me to my conversation with Edward. In my attempt to protect my heart, I have only succeeded in breaking it.

Thursday, December 29 – Phone Texts

Mindy: This sucks.

Mindy: I am amazed that you are over "us" so quickly. I aspire to follow your example. In the meantime I am beyond sad. But will try and focus on the future.

Mindy: I apologize if I seem overly melodramatic. Right now it is how I feel.

Edward: Nothing to apologize for, dear. And I'm not so easily over "us." I expected to like you. I didn't expect to like you so much. But what am I supposed to say? You said it first. You are being the adult. But I am/we are totally aware of the question. We knew it was likely a matter of when it would be said out loud.

Mindy: I am sorry to be so emotional. This is very difficult for me. It is not something that I take lightly. I love you in more than a casual live-in the-moment way.

Edward: I love you dear lady, and this is not how I want it to be, not how I want us to turn out.

Edward: I've been transcribing our texts to make room

for more. Where do they all come from?

Mindy: I figured you would be tending to that. I was reading through mine, as well. I have so enjoyed our relationship and all the parts and pieces therein. Please don't delete me too quickly.

Edward: I don't want to delete you at all, my dear. I want to keep kissing for days ... and nights!

Mindy: You have the heart of a poet.

Edward: You help inspire the poet in me, sweets.

Mindy: Sweet dreams, baby. I am thinking that celebrating the New Year together would be good closure for both of us. Let me sleep on it. Love you, too.

MINDY:

On one hand, starting the New Year with a clean slate, free of all attachments, seems the healthy way to go. But then I remember that one of my attachments is Edward, and I can't imagine not having him in my life. There is the juxtaposition of reality and fairy tale in our relationship. Feeling my feelings isn't my strong suit; I don't drink, I don't smoke, I have no way to anesthetize my breaking heart.

Edward and I talk at length about the possibility of us. We have this conversation on a regular basis. How can we make "us" work? What does that look like? Are we merely spinning a made-for-TV plot and banking on a happy ending we can't foresee at this point in time? Don't know. But I do know that I would much rather keep this reality at bay for another meeting with my sweet Edward. We understand that we are probably postponing the inevitable.

EDWARD:

Mindy and I talk on the phone this evening and we discuss spending New Year's together. We have been invited to a New Year's party at the home of part of my shag crew. It's a thoughtful invitation, but neither of us is in a public party mood. I suggest that I drive up to her house so we can visit in the peace and quiet of her lovely, organized home.

Friday, December 30 – Phone texts
Mindy: Wake up, sweets!!!

Edward: Good morning, dear heart!

Mindy: Hooooray for a long weekend! I think we should do it. If it gets too sad, we will cut it short. You are good at living in the "now" so you may have to help me.

Edward: We will celebrate the good and try to ignore the unhappy.

Mindy: We are brave on so many levels ...

Mindy: I will get cream for your coffee ... anything else?

Edward: Nooky bits for breakfast!

Mindy: I'm entirely in too good a mood. This does not bode well ...

Edward: Goose you ... gently ... cream for coffee is good. You got my supper ... I'll get din on the way ... can't think of anything else. Thank you for asking. Love you.

Mindy: I def got yo suppa. ;-)

Edward: Thank you, my brave dumpling!

Edward: Let us go with feeling good and forego the foreboding, ehh? :-*

Mindy: You may have to remind me a few times ... I am not blessed with the same hippie spirit as you, my baby. ;-)

Edward: Sweetpea ... hogs and quiches ... hugs and kisses. :-*   :-*   :-D

CHAPTER 29

Tenth Meeting
12/30/11 -1/1/12   New Year's
Mindy's House
Reston, VA

MINDY:

I know that I am vacillating between deciding to embrace Edward in my life and realizing that our relationship will maybe never work in the long haul. We are two such different people, alike and yet not. Edward and I are drawn together by the fact of our similar "live in the moment" pasts. But now, I crave certainty and stability. At least, I think I do. Logistics makes it difficult to know how we would do in the long haul. It is exhausting to live with so much doubt around my own choices.

This whole amazing experience has shown me that I am teachable and can trust my intuition. I have been honest with both myself and with Edward. He has been equally honest with me. So I know that agreeing to spend this New Year's together as our last physical meeting is just a way to prolong the inevitable pain of our final parting. Or not. I am choosing to not to think about it or take it to my comfort zone: worst case scenario. I am going to "be."

Having said that, I am excited to spend more time and start this New Year with Edward.

EDWARD:

Our tenth "One Visit Theory" and supposed to be the last.

I go visit Mindy at her home. None of society's or our personal dilemmas are solved. But we have a lovely quiet weekend together - living, laughing, and loving.

MINDY:

Our New Year's weekend is perfect. Edward and I decide to live in the moment (where Edward always lives but I very seldom even visit).

This time together is reminiscent of our very first meeting. It all flows. No talk of tomorrow, just enjoying the now -all guards down, every molecule at attention, synapses firing! We love and chatter and laugh. It is an idyllic way to start the New Year, and to celebrate the past few months of togetherness. It is the perfect homily of our love for each other.

Monday, January 2 – Phone Texts

Mindy: Thank you ... what a wondrous adventure with my baby. Love you, forever.

Edward: Love you, now, and forever, my dear.

Mindy: We are so brave.

Edward: You are the brave blurting soul who wouldn't go away when I first told you to. Thank you for that my dear.

Mindy: I don't feel brave at all right now.

Edward: You are more substantial than you give yourself

credit for. Hug you, kiss you, my dear!

Mindy: Hugs and kisses, my baby.

Edward: Mindy! Thank you for sharing the New Year with me. I don't know if I am any less confused, but thank you for sharing your time and your sweet self. I love you, dear Mindy!

Mindy: And I with you, my best baby. Thank you for sharing the start of our New Year with me. I enjoyed our time so much. I love you forever and a day!

Tuesday, January 3 - Phone Texts

Edward: Baby! Strange to think of being not with you.

Mindy: So odd to have you gone. Love my baby.

Mindy: Hate the real world. Miss our world. Kiss you.

Edward: Sweetheart. I'm not sure those are the right words but I think I understand what you mean. Kiss you back, and front.

Mindy: Note to self: I don't really hate the world; just that you and I can't be in it *together* :-)

Edward: Yes ma'am. I am in total agreement. Please let me hug and kiss you up ... and try to make it better.

MINDY:
OUR HEART

In true Edward fashion, he has decided to make his own paver stone to complete his house's relationship corner ala Feng Shui. He tells me he is going to do this. I have no idea how amazing this endeavor will turn out to be.

On a slow day at work, he begins by creating a very precise form to hold the high density cement that will be the paver heart to complete his relationship corner. As he creates the heart, he takes photos with his phone and sends them to my phone. I am beyond touched by the process of his most thoughtful creation.

Once the heart form is filled with cement, and before it dries, Edward shaves red chalk to sprinkle over the heart to give it a red hue.

EDWARD:
OUR HEART

Oh, those intriguing people of the past, astrologers for example, paying attention to the travel and interaction of the stars and heavens in our daily lives. Oh, those astute Chinese, paying attention to the flow of energy, helpful and harmful, and taking notes.

I have always seen/heard it called, "Feng Shui ... the Art Of." I am not a big fan of superstitions, but as they go, I can hang with this one, and I have no doubt it can be practiced artfully. I believe in life energy and it makes sense to have it flowing well and positively.

When Mindy came to visit me at Christmas, in my new home, we discussed the Feng Shui of the house. I have purchased and placed a variety of crystals to help the energy flow through the house. One not so minor detail is that my love/relationship corner doesn't exist in the structure of this house. That space is outside because of how the back porch doesn't go all the way across the back of the house. My love life did not exist in this house. Considering why and how I had met Mindy, and my interest in having a live and healthy love life, it isn't a good sign to move to a house with no love/relationship corner, and leave that matter unattended. The solution is to make an icon to represent that energy. Mindy and I discussed this a little and she has shared a link to a craft store that has kits for making your own tile pavers, outside type stuff. I consider it but don't really come across anything I like.

I am blessed in many ways. One of the ways is my job. I unload and load freight at a distribution center. It's unusual freight, not just pallets of goods going to the big box stores. That means that I'm on the job site 40 hours a week, but there are times when I am bravely standing by, waiting for a truck that needs attention. While I'm standing by, I have time for personal projects. And so, one of my personal projects is the creation of the icon I need to complete the love/relationship corner of my home.

I acquire a partial sheet of plywood and lay out a bit of a grid with my framing square. I cut a couple strips of cardboard 2" wide and start bending them into a heart-like shape on the plywood. Then I cut several wooden triangles from scrap wood that comes to us as dunnage under some of the freight. These triangles are screwed to the plywood as stops for the cardboard edge form. I use the parts to form a heart. High density concrete (from my collection of construction materials of my past carpentry days) is mixed and poured it into the heart form. Before the concrete completely sets up, I sprinkle carpenter's red chalk on top. This is the process of making the heart.

1. Our heart

2. Pouring in our heart

3. Our heart is full

4. Basking in the sun

5. Our heart bared to the world

See our heart in
living/loving color
at our website:
www.lubeoflife.com

EDWARD:

The mindset while working on this project starts with the help of my sweetheart, Mindy. I realize, as I begin this project, that although the finished piece is to enhance the Feng Shui of my domicile, it is actually a statement of our love for each other. Thus, it's only right to call it "Our Heart."

My dear Mindy, the woman who started in the "Cute But Too Far" folder, but refused to stay there. She became my buddy and signed up for Shag dance lessons so she could meet a nice guy. She is the sweet soul who blurted out an invitation into her life, and her love. She is the loving and lovely woman who started the wondrous adventure of "Us." I am one Lucky Duck! I am one grateful Lucky Duck! Thank you for inviting me to come along with you, Mindy, my dear!

The purpose of the heart icon is to help bring the love of my life, into my life. Or is she already here beside me, a mere two hundred miles up the highway?

MINDY:

The Curious Nature of The Universe

I am beyond moved by Edward's creation of "our heart." It occurs to me that, even though he and I valiantly try (or at least talk about trying) to meet others via our online dating and bumping up of energy via Feng Shui, what we are really doing is confusing the Universe. Or perhaps this is what is supposed to be.

Our perfect partner can't find a way to come into our lives when Edward and I are standing so close to each other. We are saying affirmations, and putting out all kinds of energy around meeting our perfect mate when, in fact, we are the ones that keep getting winked in to the space we are trying to create for someone else.

Is Edward truly the perfect partner I am looking for? Only time will tell. I have learned so much about myself in this relationship ... most especially that I am a living/breathing/feeling woman and not some desolate wasteland of aging. This realization has been huge and I am grateful for the voice inside me that told me to be brave and ask this man to be my "training wheels. "

So, dear friends, Mindy and Edward do not know how the story ends. We are still living the story as we speak, as you read…

~ To be continued ~